Neil Ormerod

INTRODUCING CONTEMPORARY THEOLOGIES

The What and the Who of Theology Today

Enlarged and Revised

E J Dwyer

First published in 1997 by
E. J. Dwyer (Australia) Pty Ltd
Unit 13, Perry Park
33 Maddox Street
Alexandria NSW 2015
Australia
Phone: (02) 9550-2355
Fax: (02) 9519-3218

National Library of Australia
Cataloguing-in-Publication data
Ormerod, Neil.
Introducing contemporary theologies: the what and the
who of theology today.

Enlarged and rev. ed.
Bibliography.
Includes index.
ISBN 0 85574 039 6.

1. Theology – History – 20th century. 2. Theologians.
I. Title.

230

Cover design by April Briscoe
Text design by Midland Typesetters
Typeset in 11 on 13pt by Midland Typesetters
Printed in the United States by Versa Press

10 9 8 7 6 5 4 3 2 1
00 99 98 97

CONTENTS

Preface   v

Part A—The *What* of Theology
  1. What is Theology?   3
  2. Philosophy and Theology   15
  3. Contemporary Theologies Compared with Previous
     Theology   27
  4. Method in Theology   42

Bibliography   58

Part B—The *Who* of Theology
  5. Hans Küng, *Making Theology Contemporary*   61
  6. Sebastian Moore, *Psychological Theology*   71
  7. Edward Schillebeeckx, *Reinterpreting the Past*   81
  8. Wolfhart Pannenberg, *Systematic Theology*   92
  9. Karl Rahner, *Transcendental Theology I*   103
 10. Bernard Lonergan, *Transcendental Theology II*   114
 11. Johann Baptist Metz, *Political Theology*   124
 12. Jürgen Moltmann, *Dialectic Theology*   134
 13. Gustavo Gutiérrez, *Liberation Theology I*   144
 14. Leonardo Boff, *Liberation Theology II*   154
 15. Elisabeth Schüssler Fiorenza, *Feminist Theology I*   164
 16. Rosemary Radford Ruether, *Feminist Theology II*   175
 17. Elizabeth Johnson, *Feminist Theology III*   185
 18. Dorothee Soëlle, *A Contemporary Theodicy*   195
 19. John Meyendorff, *Orthodox Theology*   205

Conclusion   215
Index of Names   217

ACKNOWLEDGMENTS

The author gratefully acknowledges permission to use material from "Little Gidding" in *Four Quartets*, copyright 1943 by T. S. Eliot and renewed 1971 by Esme Valerie Eliot, reprinted by permission of Harcourt Brace Jovanovich, Inc. and Faber and Faber Ltd (London).

PREFACE

In my years of studying and teaching theology I have always found contemporary theology to be both tremendously exciting and potentially disorienting. The aim, then, of this book is twofold. Firstly, I hope that I have been able to convey to the reader some of the excitement that contemporary theology can engender. Secondly, I hope that I have been able to provide the reader with, if not a map, at least a compass, so that they do not too quickly lose direction. The compass that I use is one which has got me out of difficulty on many an occasion, the theological method of Bernard Lonergan. Anyone familiar with his work will be quickly aware, on reading this book, of the debt which I owe his writings.

To fulfil this aim I have decided not on a thematic approach but one which involves a sampling of the writings of some of the leading theologians of the later half of the twentieth century. Any such sampling will involve a selection, both of the theologians and the works considered. My principles of selection have not been profound—generally a question of my own familiarity, though some were included, in particular Johann Baptist Metz and the feminists, Elisabeth Schüssler Fiorenza and Rosemary Radford Ruether, because the dynamism of the work almost demanded their inclusion. The works in general have been chosen on the criteria of readability and availability. For some theologians, of course, nothing much is readable, so compromises have had to be made. I hope that I have done them all justice.

Like all books, this one has a history. It began as a few articles in the Australian Christian social justice magazine, National Outlook, written at the invitation of a close friend,

Mauro di Nicola. The articles led to an invitation to teach a course on contemporary theology at the Strathfield campus of the Catholic College of Education, Sydney. As the course progressed and students (at least some of them!) expressed enthusiasm, I began to see the possibility of turning my notes into a proper book. With Mauro's further encouragement and the hope of a publisher, I set about my task with gusto. Though the original hope for publication faded, it was soon replaced by a firm offer from E. J. Dwyer, through the agencies of Catherine Hammond, another friend, who had recently taken up a position there.

To Mauro and Catherine go my thanks. My thanks also to those, including my wife Thea and my colleagues at St Paul's Seminary, Kensington, who read various chapters and made helpful comments. Special thanks to Denis Edwards and Margaret Jenkins, colleagues from the Australian Catholic Theological Association, who took the time and effort to read the full text and make many helpful comments and suggestions. Without the help of all these my book would have been a sad and sorry thing!

Preface to the Enlarged and Revised Edition

At the suggestion of Catherine Hammond at E. J. Dwyer, I have undertaken this enlarged and revised edition of *Introducing Contemporary Theologies*. I have used this as an opportunity to revise the first four chapters and to add five new theologians, thus expanding the focus of the original work beyond the world of Catholic theology. In particular I have added three leading Protestant theologians, Jürgen Moltmann, Wolfhart Pannenberg and Dorothee Soëlle, and a leading Orthodox theologian, John Meyendorff. Apart from some minor corrections I have left the previous chapters in Part B as they were, though I have updated the bibliographical information at the end of each chapter. Theologians continue to write new books!

I would also like to thank all those who have commented to me so favorably about the first edition. I hope that this new edition is as well received.

PART A

The *What* of Theology

In the first part of this book I consider the nature of theology, where it is coming from, what forces have and are shaping it and where it is going. Here I present both some background to and a framework for understanding contemporary theology. These four chapters provide the compass which will help the reader find her or his way through the tangled jungle that is contemporary theology. The most difficult chapter may prove to be Chapter 2, "Philosophy and Theology." If you find it tough, don't despair. Use it as a reference for terms and persons referred to later in the text.

CHAPTER 1

What is Theology?

To begin an investigation of contemporary theologies we must first have some idea of what we mean by theology. As with many questions of this type, the best way to answer is by an investigation of the subject under question, that is, the works of the theologians themselves. Indeed this is the basic premise of this book, in which I hope to introduce the reader to the work of various theologians so that the reader can have a better grasp of what theology and theologians are on about. However, at the beginning it will be helpful to have some preliminary ideas to structure our investigation.

As a starting point then, I shall begin simply with a consideration of a classical definition of theology given by St Anselm, a medieval theologian:

> Just as the right order of things demands that we first believe in the mysteries of Christian faith before daring to examine them rationally, so likewise it seems to me that, once we have been confirmed in faith, we would be neglectful if we did not then attempt **to understand what we believe** (*Cur Deus Homo*).

This is usually expressed in the shorthand formula:

> Theology is faith seeking understanding.

Apart from its brevity, this definition has some distinct advantages.

Firstly, it indicates that theology is a faith activity. It is a discipline distinct from, say, religious studies, which seeks to study religions from a neutral point of view. Theology takes a faith stance. It takes place within a faith community. It is an expression of the faith of the theologian and the community to which he or she belongs.

Secondly, it indicates the provisional nature of theology. It is seeking understanding. It does not claim to possess all understanding, but is a process which is always seeking greater understanding. A theology which does not commit itself to a continual search for understanding will quickly find itself reduced to a form of intellectual archaeology, digging into the past to revive ancient ideas, hardly aware of the distance between past and present. Partly the provisional nature of theology is due to what it studies. The mysteries of revelation are always open to greater understanding. Partly it arises from the provisional nature of understanding itself. As cultures change, what is intelligible in one may not be so in another.

Thirdly, it seeks understanding. Theology involves the use of intelligence and reason, of questioning and answering. The definition makes it clear that theology is an activity distinct from piety, authoritarianism, dogmatism and fideism (i.e. faith which rejects reason). Theology is the meeting place of faith and reason, where each must find justification in the court of the other.

In this process, understanding and reason have their own norms and criteria, which cannot be dictated to in an arbitrary way by faith. Reason demands clearly defined data, a systematic ordering of questions and judgments grounded in evidence. Once theology abandons these norms and criteria, it is reduced to a mere fideism which eventually rejoices in the irrationality of faith. Indeed, Karl Barth, a leading Protestant theologian, will claim, echoing Tertullian, an early Father of the Church, "Because it is absurd, I believe"!

Similarly, faith has its own norms and criteria which cannot be dictated to by reason. Faith recognizes an authority which goes beyond the here and now claims of our senses, beyond what we may currently think of as right and reasonable. Faith is grounded in a mystery which it claims is more that human reason can encompass. Faith accepts the particularity of God's action in human history, a particularity which may scandalize the universal claims of reason. When theology fails to recognize these norms and criteria it reduces itself to philosophy, and a merely rationalist philosophy at that.

On the other hand, there are also some disadvantages or at least unresolved questions which need to be faced in considering this definition. The following questions, while not pretending to be comprehensive, need to be addressed.

i) What are our criteria for determining faith? What is faith? Is it simply an intellectual assent to what is proposed by divine authority, as defined by Thomas Aquinas? Or does it involve a fully existential commitment, not so much of the mind but of the heart, as suggested by Martin Luther? How we understand faith will greatly influence how we do our theology.

Even more importantly, whose faith? Is the faith of a Pentecostal fundamentalist an equally valid starting point for theology as the faith of a Karl Rahner or the Pope? For Anselm, this was not a major problem. In his day there was one faith, the faith of the Church. For Anselm, there was faith, or there was heresy. There had not, at that stage, been the divisive events of the Reformation, which revealed a multiplicity of faiths, each claiming to be the true inheritor of the Christian faith. What criteria do we use to distinguish between these various expressions of Christian faith, or between an authentic or an unauthentic Christianity?

Here also, we can appreciate the fact that faith is not an individual possession but an ecclesial reality, something belonging to the Church (*ecclesia*) as a whole. Faith grows out of a community and creates new community. Faith identifies with a living tradition. A theologian, seeking to understand faith, does so as a member of an ecclesial community and is often supported in that task by the community. There are mutual rights and responsibilities between theologians and Church which inevitably lead to tension between the two. The theologian has the right to raise questions, to examine issues, which may unsettle the less reflective faith of the community.

On the other hand, the community has the right to define, i.e. set limits to, its own faith, to pass judgment on whether a particular understanding is in fact part of its belief. In the early Church this process of passing judgment was often undertaken by a general Council, such as the Council of Nicea (325 CE), which defined the divinity of Jesus. In the Catholic Church at present this process is usually part of the role of the magisterium, or official teaching body of the Church, the bishops and the Pope acting in unison. Yet such actions are meant to be reflective of the faith of the whole Church, the *sensus fidelium*. Other Christian Churches too have their own mechanisms for setting limits on what is acceptable and what is not acceptable for a Christian theologian to say. Such limits define our identity as churches, in much the same way that geographical borders identify nations.

ii) The definition assumes that *faith* is amenable to *understanding* and reason. While the Catholic tradition has long held that this is so, is it not an assumption that needs to be investigated? We need to inquire thoroughly whether and in what senses faith is reasonable.

One difficulty here is that if we require that faith be reasonable, does this not determine the outcome of our theology before we even start? The problem is that what we consider reasonable determines the structure of our faith and so determines the way we understand our faith. On the other hand, a common human experience is that the demands of faith can be such as to bring into question that which had previously been considered reasonable. As St Paul said, Christian faith appeared as folly to the Greeks who were seeking wisdom (I Corinthians 1:20). If we allow our prior determinations of what is or is not reasonable to evaluate our faith, then why bring faith in at all? Why not just speak of "reason seeking understanding" and call it philosophy? Indeed the whole question of the relationship between theology and philosophy will be a regular theme in this book.

iii) Is understanding an absolute or a relative category? Does an understanding which arises in one person, one age, one culture, one society apply to all persons, ages, cultures and societies? It is clear that the medieval theologians, particularly Thomas Aquinas, achieved a remarkable intellectual synthesis of Christian faith. However, we have to ask, if once an understanding such as the Scholastic synthesis has been achieved, is there no more work to be done on the issue ever again? Does theology then become simply an historical investigation of understandings from the past? Or is an understanding appropriate to the medieval mind one which is simply relative to the

age, the culture, the society? Do we need to seek new understandings relative to our own age, culture and society? We have
to keep in mind that what one person in one culture finds intelligible can often be quite unintelligible to someone in another.
For example, an appeal to family honor will be quite intelligible
to someone from an Eastern culture, but much less intelligible
to a Western mind. Can, does and should theology seek some
absolute type of understanding, if such is possible, or can it be
satisfied with the relative?

The question of understanding invites some comparison
between theology and empirical science. Empirical science, at
least in its modern self-understanding, also claims to be a discipline devoted to understanding. Science is theoretical, empirical, inductive, not definitive, indeed often denying the
possibility of some type of definitive understanding. Does theology seek understanding in the same way that science does?
Should theology model itself on the empirical sciences, or does
it have its own particular methodology? Aquinas held that theology is a science, yet his understanding of what constitutes
science would no longer fit the self-understanding of modern
empirical science. What then are the differences and similarities
between the methods of theology and modern science? Further,
if their methods are similar, does the difference reside simply
in the data to which they attend or are there other factors that
need to be taken into account?

iv) If theology is defined as "faith seeking understanding"
can it ever make "truth claims," i.e. can it claim to be objective?
Surely faith is subjective, a personal commitment, which rules
out any possibility of objectivity? If this is the case, then what
criteria can we use to say "this is good/bad theology," "this is
true/false in a theological sense"? Surely it is just a matter of
"personal taste"? In what way can objectivity and truth be
claimed when the starting point is faith? On the other hand,
both the Churches, in the form of the magisterium or some
other mechanism, and the theological academy, through peer
review, are often called on to make such judgments. What then
do such judgments mean?

In particular, one might consider those judgments made by
the early Church Councils, which became official dogmas of
Christian faith. Such judgments appear to make a claim to truth,

to be more than statements of relative importance, relative to a particular history and culture. Such judgments make a claim to absoluteness in a sea of relativity. Do such judgments, in fact, make absolute claims on the theologian? Do they place artificial limits on the questions that the theologian can ask? Or do they represent a legitimate limit, defined by the community, on what is constitutive of its faith?

A good example of this type of issue is that of the ordination of women. Pope John Paul II has made a judgment, which, while not invoking his full authority, appears to bind the Catholic Church to a certain position. In doing so he is making a claim that the failure of the Church to ordain women in the past is not the result of social and cultural forces, but rather the result of the will of Jesus Christ. Catholic theologians are presently struggling to grasp the significance of this claim. In many ways it represents the tension between the absolute and the relative, between authority and reason, between obedience and evidence. Other Churches, such as the Anglican and Episcopalian communions, have struggled with the same issue and come to a different conclusion. This raises again the ecclesial nature of theology.

Such questions reflect an ongoing tension within the theological community. In the theologians studied in this book we shall see a variety of stances with regard to the problem posed by dogmas, from radical rejection to critical acceptance. Here the comparison with the empirical sciences exacerbates the problem. Certainty and truth have become marginal categories in modern sciences, which seek, not definitive truth, but better understanding. In an age where empirical science tends to become a paradigm for all knowledge, claims to an absolute truth, as embodied in a dogma, seem either arrogance or an authoritarian dogmatism from the past.

Yet there are fundamental differences between the empirical sciences and theology. Traditionally, faith has seen the definitiveness of dogma not as a human achievement but as a divine gift, a revelation from God. Theology, as a faith activity, may need to recognize the possibility of a definitive breakthrough into the realm of truth, which is simply not attainable within the empirical sciences. We shall consider this again in Chapter 4 and in the various theologians we shall study.

v) If we place our emphasis on understanding, does theology become a purely "theoretical" study? Does it live in an academic world of "pure theory" in its own ivory tower, or does it impact on the world and Church in practical ways? Theology is a form of activity, an action within the ecclesial community which history shows has implications for the life of the Church. Indeed theology has at times played an important role in clarifying the Church community's self-understanding. At other times, dominant theologies have acted as straitjackets, limiting the Church community's self-understanding and protecting the vested interests of those who wield authority within the community.

Does our definition perhaps act to conceal this fact from view, hoping to make theology "politically neutral"? On the other hand, if we acknowledge the impact that theology has on Church life, then what place does praxis, committed action/reflection, have in theology? This is a question that has been raised most recently in Liberation and Political Theologies.

These are just some of the issues raised by the classical definition. As I said above, they do not pretend to be comprehensive. On the other hand, many of them go to the heart of the contemporary debate concerning the nature of theology. During the course of this book I hope that the reader will see many of these questions again in the context of particular theologies. Perhaps it will be only then that the reader will be able to appreciate the implications of the issues I have raised above.

The Psychological Analogy: A Classic Example of Faith Seeking Understanding

Belief in the Trinity is central to Christian faith. In many ways it is the quintessential Christian mystery, something only known because of revelation. It tells us something not just about how God deals with humanity, but something about divinity itself. In his classical work, *De Trinitate*, Augustine, accepting the truth of the doctrine, sought to understand it. To do so he developed an analogy for the processions of the Son from the Father and the Spirit from the Father and the Son in terms of the human psychological operations for knowing and willing. The purpose of this analogy was simply to try to understand, if only in a limited way, the truths of faith. It did not try to prove the doctrine, or even try to provide evidence for it. It simply sought to render the doctrine intelligible. This analogy was given more precise metaphysical exposition by Thomas Aquinas in the *Summa Theologiae*.

The classical definition of Anselm sought to capture the irreducible essence of theology. However, as I have argued above, it raises as many questions as it answers. As an alternative to this classical definition, we might consider the following functional definition taken from the work of Bernard Lonergan, one of the theologians we shall consider later:

> Theology mediates between a cultural matrix and the significance and role of a religion in that matrix.
>
> (B. Lonergan, *Method in Theology*, p.xi.)

(Here the term "cultural matrix" refers to the meanings, values, structures, institutions and so on which constitute and perpetuate the culture.) This definition is functional in the sense that it seeks to describe the function of theology, rather than try to capture its essence. It seeks to tell us what theology does rather than what it is. As an alternative, it helps us shed light on some of the issues that were raised by the classical definition of Anselm. However, it also raises questions and issues which are fruitful to consider.

Firstly, we must ask what do we mean by culture—do we have a normative or an empirical notion of culture? A normative definition of culture takes one culture, usually Western European culture, as the norm by which all other cultures are to be judged. One either lives up to the standards set by this culture, in which case one is considered civilized, or one fails to live up to it, in which case one is considered a barbarian (or a child, or a woman!). Here it is interesting to note that the Apostolic Constitution on the first Code of Canon Law, issued by Benedict XV in 1917, saw one of the goals of the Catholic

Church to be bringing culture to the barbarians! Indeed missionaries of all persuasions have usually brought more than just the Gospel with them, usually imposing aspects of Western culture upon new converts.

Within the confines of a normative notion of culture, theology will be seen as a permanent achievement, a lasting accomplishment. The sole task of later generations will be to stand in awe at the achievement of the past. Any variation from its canons will be seen as a sure sign of decadence and imminent collapse.

Alternatively, one may have an empirical notion of culture. Here, a culture is seen as a set of meanings and values which inform and structure a way of life. One then compares and contrasts cultures, evaluates their weaknesses and strengths, studies how they give meaning and purpose to people's lives. No one culture can be seen as a definitive and permanent achievement, since all are open to development and change, progress as well as decline.

Given an empirical notion of culture, theology can be seen to be an ongoing process. Here, theology is located as an activity within a culture. As culture changes, so will theology. A theology that is suitable for a medieval culture will not necessarily be suitable for contemporary culture, since the basic thought forms, the meanings which inform a culture, can be quite different.

For example, medieval theology made fundamental use of a static hierarchical ontology, or conception of being. Such a static hierarchical structure was self-evident to the medieval mind— society was a static hierarchy, the Church was a static hierarchy, so of course being was a static hierarchy. Within our own culture, static hierarchy has been replaced by dynamic evolving process. Such different cultural starting-points will give rise to markedly different theologies. If we wish to make a comparison between the two, we must look not only at their conclusions but also at such fundamental starting-points.

Lonergan's functional definition also raises other questions. I noted above that culture can change theology. Can theologies change cultures? Or can theologies act in such a way as to justify cultures? In the example above, about the medieval notion of a hierarchy of being, not only does the medieval culture make such a conception more plausible, but once the ontology is accepted as true, it, in its turn, acts as a justifying principle for the hierarchical structuring of society. Being is hierarchical, therefore society and Church should be hierarchical! In this way theology may act as an ideological justification for a given social and political system. One could ask similar questions about our contemporary uncritical acceptance of a dynamic evolving ontology. May it not also serve an ideological function, justifying certain social forces which need more critical attention?

Part of what we are doing here is drawing attention to the fact that the mediation between religion and culture is a two-way street. Theology mediates meaning and value from culture to religion and from religion to culture. Religion is not presumed to have all the answers—it must also listen to culture. Good examples of this are in the area of human rights in general, and women's rights in particular. Here, culture has largely taken the lead in defining human rights and recognizing, in particular, the way women have been systematically denied rights in society. The Catholic Church has been slow to recognize and act on rights which are now taken for granted in secular societies, for example, the right to due process. Part of the theological task is to help mediate such values to the Church, to recognize the truly human on which grace must build.

Modern Feminism: An Example of the Mediation between Culture and Religion

Many conservative Christians see Christianity and the modern feminist movement as sworn enemies. Yet modern feminism had its origins in the Christian churches. In the USA the suffragette movement grew out of the involvement of Christian women in the anti-slavery, abolitionist struggle. These women began to see parallels between their own situation and that of the slaves, both in society and in the Church. They even saw the right of women to ministry as a higher priority than gaining the vote! While the feminist movement had major successes in the secular sphere, the slowness of the Churches in responding forced many feminists out of the Christian community. Feminism became more and more a secular movement. Now that movement is again impacting upon the Churches through the work of feminist theologians and biblical scholars. The mediation has gone full circle from religion to culture and back again to religion.

Within our contemporary society we also have to ask what are the mechanisms by which culture listens to religion. In the medieval world, working in a conception of society as Christendom, the channels of communication from religion to culture were clear and well defined. In our contemporary, secular society, religion has become a marginalized, privatized activity, something to be done between consenting adults. Since the advent of the Enlightenment and the secularism that it espoused, religion has been struggling to find a place within society. The traditional authority of religion has all but been eroded away. Again this puts out a massive challenge to theology. The audience of theology should not be just the ecclesial community, but also the culture at large. The theologian has to find ways of engaging secular culture in debate. Such an engagement cannot be on the basis of a presupposed divine authority which is no longer accepted, but on the basis of the authority of competence, an intellectual mastery of the issues on which the theologian can bring to bear the wisdom of the Christian tradition.

Conclusion

This brief discussion is meant simply to get the reader thinking about the nature and purpose of theology. In it I have raised several issues—what is the relationship between faith and reason, or more specifically theology and philosophy? What is an appropriate methodology for theology and how does its method relate to other methods such as scientific method? What is the relationship between theology and culture? When we look at the various theologians studied in this book, I hope to bring out the way in which each relates to these basic questions and what comments they have to make on the issues involved.

DISCUSSION QUESTIONS

- How do you see the relationship between theology and Christian doctrine?

- How do you understand scientific method? What comparisons would you draw between scientific and theological method?

- Discuss ways in which religion may influence culture and culture may influence religion.

CHAPTER 2

Philosophy and Theology

In the previous chapter I raised the question of the relationship between theology and philosophy. Historically, there has always been a close connection between philosophy and theology, though this was seriously challenged during the Reformation and remains a point of tension between Catholic and Protestant theologians (though there are notable exceptions such as Paul Tillich and, more recently, Wolfhart Pannenberg). Catholic tradition has always held a special place for the Christianization of Aristotle achieved by Thomas Aquinas. Indeed, it was christened the perennial philosophy. The Thomistic synthesis, however, has not been the only philosophical influence on theology. There have been many and varied influences, ancient and modern. An outline of contemporary theology cannot ignore the major philosophical influences that have operated in theology. To attempt to do so would be to give a distorted, incomplete picture.

Many may find the material in this chapter difficult to grasp. The problem is that philosophers ask questions which most people find irrelevant and even annoying—What is reality? How do we know? What is the relationship between knowing and reality? While the majority of us can spend most of our lives never worrying about such questions, they become important once one attempts to systematically understand one's faith. For example, if a Catholic wants to talk about the "real presence" of Christ in the Eucharist, it may be important to know what one means by "real." Philosophy helps to get it straight, if not necessarily to get it right!

This connection between theology and philosophy should not surprise us. To express itself in a systematic way, theology needs to either draw on or create categories which express the realities with which it deals. Since this includes the realities of the "mundane" world, and philosophy already attempts to provide such categories for the "mundane" world, theology will draw on these. For example, the Council of Nicea found it necessary to use the category of *substance* (in Greek, *ousia*) in order to define the relationship between Jesus and the Father (in the Creed we say that the Father and Son are of one substance or being). Such a use of philosophy may be naive or critical, explicit or implicit. Experience has shown that the naive and implicit adoption of a philosophical system often leads to a confused and uncritical theology. Philosophy is useful in any systematic process of understanding, since it helps uncover gaps and prejudices which would otherwise remain unexamined.

Recently, theology has attempted to integrate not only philosophy but also many of the human sciences into its world view. Theologians must now be acquainted with psychology, sociology, even economics, as well as with philosophy. Bernard Lonergan has argued that the human sciences must also become acquainted with theology, though this has not received a warm response from these sciences. Some theologians believe that the human sciences can even replace philosophy in some sense. However, I would argue that philosophy remains an essential element in the theologian's armory, since only philosophy can provide an integrative framework for all the sciences, human and empirical. Philosophy provides a total, if open-ended, heuristic, world view, for which the particular sciences provide the concrete instances.

The other important thing to realize in investigating the various philosophers is that, whether we like it or not, they have shaped our present Western culture. Their thoughts, even their language, have become a part of our heritage and the way we argue. One need only note that the Britannica *Great Books of the Western World* contains a sizable contribution from philosophers.

Without going into great detail, it would be advantageous, therefore, to look at some of the major philosophical influences which have been operating in contemporary theology. Below I shall give "thumb-nail sketches" of the various philosophers and their philosophies. Such sketches are possible only on the assumption that the reader is not a professional philosopher, who would undoubtedly be annoyed by the descriptions I shall give. We shall encounter these various philosophies when we deal with the work of particular theologians.

I shall begin with two ancient but most significant philosophers, Plato and Aristotle. Some would say that these two provide all philosophy with its basic themes and tensions. Then I shall consider more recent philosophers who, I feel, have contributed in significant ways to the development of contemporary theology.

Plato: 428-348 BCE (approx.)

No account of philosophy could afford to leave out Plato. His system of thought is not only powerful, but also simple and easily popularized. Plato contrasted the ephemeral changing world of the senses with the unchanging world of truth and ideas. For Plato, this unchanging world of ideas was reality and the ephemeral world of the senses was simply a shadowy reflection of the ideas. These, such as the idea of man, the idea of the good, were substantial in some sense, and existed in some "heavenly" realm. In this system of thought, perfection and knowledge were attained through contemplation of the higher ideas, the good, the true, the beautiful. In this way, the human person could rise above brutish nature. Technically, Plato's philosophy is known as a type of idealism, because it sees the realm of ideas as more real that that of the senses. It is also referred to as a form of dualism, which identifies matter and spirit as distinct substances.

Many Christians operate out of a naive Platonic dualism—matter-spirit, body-soul, heaven-earth. Plato's work has had a significant influence through its assimilation by Augustine into his major synthesis of Christian theology. However, as a philosophical position, this Platonic dualism finds it difficult to give expression to, say, the resurrection of the body. For Plato, death frees the soul which had been trapped in the body, frees it to contemplate the ideas. In such a view, a resurrected body is simply another trap for the soul, tying it down to the material once again.

Aristotle: 384-322 BCE

The other major figure from the philosophical past that we must meet is Aristotle. A pupil of Plato, Aristotle sought to "bring Plato's ideas down to earth." Aristotle maintained a "moderate realism"—the realm of ideas is not divorced nor ontologically separated from the material world, but is immanent within it. Rather than ideas, he spoke of the form of the object. This form was the intelligibility of the object, grasped by the intellect in the data presented by the senses. The form "informed" the matter to constitute the object, to make it what it is. For Aristotle, knowledge comes not from contemplation but through inquiry. Indeed, he lived this out, writing not only in philosophy, but also in the natural sciences backed by empirical observations.

Aristotle has also had a major impact on Christian theology. His concepts of form, matter, act, potency, become part of the Christian heritage through the work of Aquinas. In the twelfth century, the works of Aristotle were "rediscovered" by the Western world through the agency of Moslem invaders moving up through southern Europe. Aquinas rapidly adopted (and adapted) the Aristotelian categories in his Christian theology, gaining for his efforts the wrath of his contemporaries, who depended heavily on Platonic philosophy. During his lifetime Aquinas' writings were condemned, and it was only after his death that he was restored to favor and eventually canonized. This is a good illustration of how philosophical differences can lead to theological conflict.

These two imposing figures from ancient times provide a backdrop to all philosophy. We shall now turn our attention to some more modern (post-Renaissance) figures, who have influenced contemporary theology.

Kant: 1724-1804

Kant developed his philosophy in reaction to the empiricism of David Hume and as an attempt to find a philosophical justification for the success of the empirical sciences. He distinguished between the phenomenal aspects of an object (appearance) and the noumenal (the thing-in-itself). The senses put us in touch with the phenomenal, while the noumenal is in a sense unknowable. The mind then processes the data of sense by applying *a priori* categories of thought to arrive at what we call knowledge. However, it is not knowledge of the *noumena*, the real thing-in-itself, but simply a projection of human understanding onto the object.

Kant arrived at these a *priori* categories through a process known as a "transcendental deduction." This consists of a deduction which begins with a question of the type "what are the *a priori* conditions for the possibility of ... sense experience?" Here *a priori* refers to prior, given structures or contents within the knowing subject. It is what we bring to the object as knowing subjects as opposed to what the object presents to us, the *a posteriori*. Such *a priori* structures are called "transcendental." As a result Kant's system is often called "transcendental idealism."

In raising the question of the role of the subject in knowing, Kant brings to the fore the whole problem of objectivity. If prior structures within the subject are important factors in coming to know, in what sense can my knowledge be "objective"? Surely if my knowledge is to be objective, it must be determined solely by the object, without any *a priori* contribution from the subject. Such difficult questions lie at the heart of the problematic set by Kant for succeeding generations of philosophers.

Indeed we can witness these difficulties in many modern debates and conversations. How often do we hear people say something like, "That's just your interpretation. I interpret it differently"? Such an assertion basically follows Kant's belief that we project concepts onto reality. Different people may project different concepts or interpretations onto the same events or things, but the thing-in-itself is beyond our knowing. A more realist position than Kant's might ask whether a given interpretation is correct. But this assumes that the event or thing has its own meaning independent of our concepts. Only if this is the case can we say that a particular interpretation is false.

In his *Critique of Pure Reason*, Kant claims that there are three things which it is impossible to know, three noumenal realities—the existence of God, the immortality of the soul, and the existence of human freedom. On the other hand, these three are the basic assumptions of practical reason, the grounds of morality. His moral philosophy puts great stress on duty. In one way or another, these three questions shape much of modern theology.

We shall see further evidence of Kant's influence later on, particularly the use of the "transcendental deduction," in the work of Karl Rahner. Both Karl Rahner and Bernard Lonergan have been labelled "transcendental Thomists," where the tag "transcendental" refers to the influence of Kant or his methodology.

Hegel: 1770-1831

Hegel is a most difficult thinker. He sought to develop a complete system which would encompass everything, a total, absolute "Idea." His aim was to explain not only knowledge but history as well, in particular the history of philosophy. Hegel hoped to develop a philosophy of philosophies, a comprehensive system which would explain and encompass all other philosophical systems. The dynamic of the system was dialectic, the dialectic of thesis, antithesis and synthesis. This synthesis then becomes the new thesis evoking antithesis and so on to ever greater syntheses. Indeed, this new system would be so all-encompassing that it would embrace and replace religion. Hegel held Christianity in high esteem, since it is a religion of the "spirit," but still it was to be replaced by his philosophy of the "spirit."

In one area Hegel's philosophy gives us a major breakthrough. For the first time, history becomes an important philosophical category. But Hegel's history is still idealized, formal rather than concrete. Politically, it was used as an ideological bolster for the Prussian state, which was seen as the social counterpart to Hegel's system. Hegel's philosophy, along with those of Fichte and Schelling, were part of "German Idealism."

Hegel also gave us what is called the "master-slave" dialectic. In this he examines the relationship between oppressor and oppressed, how the slave grows to experience his dignity through his relationship with the master, how this threatens the master, and how the master is himself enslaved by his dependency on and fear of the slave. In the hands of Marx, this will be the model of class struggle.

German Idealism has had a significant influence on contemporary theologies, particularly those touched by German culture. Those influenced by Hegel include Karl Barth and Karl Rahner, as well as the more contemporary works of Hans Kung and Wolfhart Pannenberg.

Marx: 1818-1883

Few philosophers can claim to have had as great an impact on world history as Karl Marx. Though greatly influenced by Hegel, Marx turns Hegel on his head. Rather than the driving force of history being found in the "Idea," Marx locates it in matter, in particular in the economic infrastructure of society. It is this economic infrastructure, the means of production, which determines the social and cultural levels. Here Hegel's dialectic of ideas "falls over" into a dialectic materialism. Marx's history is not the history of ideas, but the history of class struggle, whereby the proletariat seeks to take over the means of production, wresting it from the hands of the capitalists, and so to create a communist state.

Marx's breakthrough was to indicate the economic and social forces which shape our thinking. He uncovers the "false consciousness" of ideology inherent in the programs of Hegel and Kant. For Marx, the root of "false consciousness" is private property, so that the destruction of false consciousness can be achieved through the abolition of private property and the placing of all property into the hands of the state. Private property is a symptom of alienation, the alienation of the worker from what he produces. Indeed, Marx defines property as alienated labor. Negatively, Marx reduces everything to questions of economic processes, with no regard to the positive contributions of the human spirit. Marx's thought operates between two poles, a scientific Marxism which is deterministic in character and a humanistic Marxism which stresses commitment to social change. There is clearly an unresolved tension between these two.

Another key element in Marx's philosophy is his commitment to political action or praxis. For Marx, the point of philosophy is not simply to understand the movements of history but to change history itself. In this way philosophy becomes political as it seeks to change the social structures which it analyzes. On this criterion one would have to judge Marx to have been quite successful, since few philosophers have had as significant an influence on historical events as Karl Marx!

While one may not expect Marx's philosophy to have had much influence on theology, Liberation Theology has found in Marx a rich source of ideas. It was this flirtation with Marxism which led to criticism of Liberation Theology from the Sacred Congregation for the Doctrine of the Faith. We shall refer again to this in the chapter on Gustavo Gutiérrez.

Existentialism

Existentialism is as much a literary as a philosophical movement. Certainly the literary works of Albert Camus and Jean Paul Sartre are more frequently read than their purely philosophical works. Still, they have made an important contribution to modern philosophy, as has the German existentialist, Martin Heidegger. Existentialism places great stress on the importance of the individual confronting the decisions and conflicts of life. It attempts a return to the concrete situation of the subject, but tends to conceive of the subject in individualistic terms—for Sartre, "hell is other people"; for Camus the basic philosophical question is whether or not to commit suicide! On the other hand, existentialism introduced important human experiences into the philosophical dialogue—dread, guilt, anguish.

Existentialism was introduced into the theological agenda by, among others, Rudolph Bultmann, who attempted an existential exegesis of the New Testament—the famous program of demythologization. In this program Bultmann sought to strip the New Testament message of what he considered its mythological content, its images of heaven and hell, of miracles and wonders. For Bultmann, faith was an existential act, an encounter with Christ which leads to the decision of faith. Paul Tillich, Karl Rahner and John Macquarrie have all been significantly influenced by the existentialist philosphy of Martin Heidegger.

Hermeneutic Philosophy

This branch of modern philosophy focuses on the questions and problems of meaning—the creation of meaning, the transmission of meaning, the interpretation of meaning. How do we mediate the meanings of the past, in the form of scripture, literature, art, beliefs, practices, to the present? How much does the interpreter influence the interpretation? What is the significance of a tradition of interpretation, particularly of classical texts such as the Bible? Significant contributions have been made in this area by Paul Ricoeur, Hans-Georg Gadamer and Jürgen Habermas. While these questions arose out of a general investigation of the human situation, they have obvious importance in theology and scriptural exegesis. Faith, Church community, and theology are about the handing of meanings and values from one generation to the next. A proper understanding of hermeneutics is essential in the contemporary theological setting.

Hermeneutic philosophy is renowned for its introduction of a "hermeneutics of suspicion and of recovery," and the "hermeneutic circle." A hermeneutics of suspicion is an interpretative process which seeks the sources of meaning in the baser human motivations. Ricoeur calls Marx, Nietzsche and Freud the masters of suspicion. Marx reduces everything to economic motives, Nietzsche to the will to power, and Freud to the urges of the subconscious. A hermeneutics of recovery, on the other hand, seeks to restore meaning as the product of human creativity.

The notion of the hermeneutic circle has varied uses. It can refer to the interaction of subject and object in the interpretative process. It can refer to the process whereby to interpret a literary work one must understand each of its components, while to understand each of its components one must understand the whole of the work.

Many theologies have, in fact, drawn upon the ideas of hermeneutics. Liberation and feminist theologies have made use of a hermeneutics of suspicion. The key doctrine of Liberation Theology, the preferential option for the poor, suggests that we should look at history from the view of the poor and marginalized, and is suspicious that many histories and theologies are written from the perspective of the rich and powerful. Feminist Theology is suspicious that Christian texts have been infiltrated by patriarchy. American theologian David Tracy has adopted ideas of Gadamer in his references to Christian classic texts. Nearly all theologians would recognize the need to develop hermeneutic principles for the interpretation of scripture and Church dogmas.

Process Philosophy

Process philosophy is the creation of Alfred Whitehead, with antecedents in the philosophy of Hegel and Henri Bergson. It is basically a metaphysical philosophy, concentrating on the question of the nature of reality rather than the person. Its key category is that of process, by which it seeks to overcome what is seen to be the static metaphysics of classical Christian philosophy. Instead of being, it speaks of creative becoming and so it understands reality as a process of continual creative unfolding. Even God is understood to be in process, so that God also changes. According to process thought, not only does God affect the world, but the world affects God, and so elicits from God a creative response.

Because of its dynamic understanding of reality, process philosophy can easily come to grips with an evolutionary worldview. Indeed it arose as a response to the changing worldviews that evolution brought to the modern world. Process thought is one of the few fundamentally metaphysical approaches to be found in contemporary theology.

The impact of process thought has been greatest in North America, due to its adoption by theologians such as David Tracy, John Cobb and Schubert Ogden. In Australia, the scientist and environmentalist Charles Birch has been highly influenced by process thought. Others, such as Jürgen Moltmann, have attempted a theology of the Trinity using process ideas. However, it has not been without its critics. Many, including Pannenberg, have strongly rejected it, claiming that process thought is not compatible with the Christian doctrine of God as creator. They fear that it unnecessarily compromises the divine transcendence. It remains a significant, if somewhat controversial, contributor to contemporary theologies.

These are the main philosophical approaches which will be mentioned. You will probably need to refer back to these pages as we proceed through the book. Other approaches will be mentioned as and when needed.

Conclusion

It is time to make some general observations about the various philosophies above. The classical philosophies of Plato and Aristotle were metaphysical in nature, i.e. their primary focus was on the object, on reality. Their basic question is: "what is being?" They sought the most general answer to this most general question. Modern philosophies, since the time of Descartes, have focused more and more, not on the object, but on the subject, on the human person, on philosophical anthropology (an exception to this is clearly process philosophy).

In general, philosophy swings between these two poles of subject and object, the subject who knows and the object that is known. Since the time of Kant, who claimed to initiate a "Copernican revolution" in philosophy, we have been made aware of how object and subject mutually condition and are conditioned by each other. The nature of this mutual conditioning is a central problem for both philosophy and theology. It is the recognition of this problem and attempts to solve it which have earned contemporary philosophy the label "critical." Any philosophy or theology which ignores this difficulty is uncritical or naive.

Put simply, we need to face the question of what it means when we say "this is true" or "this is good." Such judgments are the judgments of a human subject. Different subjects often make different judgments. Does this imply that such statements are merely subjective? Or is there the possibility of the human subject transcending mere subjectivity and actually saying something meaningful about the object, about reality? If so, what are the criteria within the subject which ground an authentic, objective judgment of fact or value? This is the debate initiated by Kant and one with which contemporary theology is still struggling. We shall see many instances of it in the chapters to come.

DISCUSSION QUESTIONS

- How do you see the relationship between philosophy and theology?

- What dangers and advantages do you see in this relationship?

CHAPTER 3

Contemporary Theologies Compared with Previous Theology

To write a book on contemporary theologies is to assume that contemporary theologies differ from the theology of previous generations. Nowhere is this more true than with Catholic theology. While Protestant theology developed in a more "dialectical" manner, Catholic theology locked itself into a very defensive position after the Reformation and the Enlightenment. Catholic theology cut itself off from the intellectual ferment that was taking place in the wider culture. As a result, when change eventually did catch up with it, it did so with a bang. Much of the upheaval in recent Catholicism can be traced to the retarded intellectual development which was forced upon the Catholic Church through its own defensiveness. What had occurred was a breakdown in the connections between religion and culture, from which it is still recovering.

The task now at hand is to examine what some of these differences are between contemporary theology and the theology from which it immediately diverged. In the case of Catholic theology, this previous theology dominated the nineteenth century, though its roots go back much further and unfortunately its branches reached well into the twentieth century.

Catholic Theology in the Nineteenth Century

It is not my intention to give a detailed analysis of the Catholic theology of the nineteenth century. Nor would I be capable of doing so. However, from the reading I have done I would characterize the theology of the previous century by the following terms.

Metaphysical

The key language of this theology was metaphysics, or the philosophy of being. The metaphysics used was a blend of Platonic and Aristotelian concepts. Being was conceived in static and hierarchical terms, truth was fixed and immutable and generally held to be in possession.

Within this theological system, classical theological problems were solved by uses of metaphysical categories of essence, existence, substance, potency, act, habit. Thus the question of the real presence of Christ in the Eucharist was dealt with by speaking of transubstantiation, a change in substance. The classical definition of the Council of Chalcedon, that Christ is one person with two natures, was dealt with by distinguishing between the existence and the essence of an object. Grace was defined as a supernatural entitative habit (i.e. a permanent quality added to and above nature modifying the very being of the thing).

Coming to grips with this metaphysical system was a basic prerequisite for studying theology! On the positive side, the use of metaphysics was an attempt to find a mode of expression which was "transcultural," which transcended cultural limitations. Being is universally accessible, so that debate about being can hope to find some type of common ground in all cultures.

Scholastic

Though this became a term of abuse, the scholastic methodology was simply to raise and answer questions in a systematic manner. Typically the question was posed, objections were noted, an authority was cited and then the matter was resolved. The classical exponent on this approach is the *Summa Theologiae* of Thomas Aquinas. Every article begins with a question, cites a number of authorities that would indicate a particular answer, cites a single reference which refutes them, then proceeds to give a reasoned response, together with answers to objections. This process continues for hundreds of pages!

The line of questions was to find greater precision, e.g. when was the precise moment when bread and wine became the Body and Blood of Christ. However, there seemed to be a lack of discernment concerning the importance of various questions. Thomas spent as much time discussing esoteric questions about angels as about central areas of faith. The method fell into disrepute, the standard jibe being that the scholastics used to ask how many angels could dance on the head of a pin. I have never seen any proof that Thomas Aquinas ever in fact asked this question!

Clearly, this style of theology predates the nineteenth century by hundreds of years. Its persistence as a method is indicative both of its conceptual clarity and of the failure of theology to come to grips with a changing intellectual climate.

Ahistorical

History was not of major concern to theology. This is true in two senses.

Firstly, as a source of theological matter, history was treated in a compressed, ahistorical manner. Theology's concern was simply to uncover what the various authorities had said—Church Councils, early Fathers—in an almost fundamentalist way. There was little sensitivity to the changing contexts and meanings that history gives rise to. Indeed, many of the problems that the scholastic method, discussed above, tried to solve arose precisely because of a lack of sensitivity to the problem of meaning. There was often a failure to realize that words used in one culture at one time could mean something quite different in another culture and time. The assumption that they did have the same meaning gave rise to great difficulties.

Secondly, as a category, history was not significant. Theology was seen as dealing with eternal truths, not with historical contingencies. This was largely a result of the static metaphysics that was employed. Within this system, change was somehow seen as suspect, as proof of error or imperfection.

To give some examples of the impact of this on theology, eschatology (the theology concerned with the definitive state of human existence) was seen in ahistorical privatized terms, something that happens "when I die" and "when the world ends." Similarly, revelation was a set of revealed truths of divine realities, rather than related to a series of concrete historical events, centering on the life, death and resurrection of Jesus and resulting in the offer of salvation to all peoples.

A sad example of the lack of significance given to history occurred at the First Vatican Council (1869-70). During the debate on papal infallibility, some of the Bishops expressed concern about various historical anomalies, such as papal statements, which were a bit embarrassing. Others claimed that the proclamation of papal infallibility would solve any historical problems! (For an account of the events at Vatican I, based on the first-hand diaries and letters of Bishop Ullathorne, see *The Vatican Council* by Dom Cuthbert Butler, Longmans, 1930.)

Dogmatic

Again, theology was dogmatic in two senses. Firstly, it was concerned with establishing and defending the dogmas of the Church, and the concept of dogma itself. This is especially clear in the canons of Vatican I. Particular dogmas, such as transubstantiation, papal infallibility, the assumption of Mary, had always been a sore point between Catholics and Protestants. However, the very notion of dogma had also come under attack with the Enlightenment, which saw it as against human dignity to have a truth imposed upon it, to be accepted purely on the basis of extrinsic authority.

Secondly, this process of establishment and defence within theology was dogmatic, i.e. obtained by an appeal to authority. For example, scripture was used in proof-text fashion, taking texts out of their context, without due regard for the meaning intended by their authors. Often in difficult cases, arguments were settled by weighing up opposing authorities. This led to a definite lack of creativity in theology.

At its worst, such a theology degenerated into a form of positivism, sometimes called Denzinger theology, named after the standard reference to the pronouncements of Church Councils and the Popes. Such a theology sought to make logical deductions from a set of "axioms" provided by scripture and Church dogmas. Method gave way to logic—a good tool but a poor master. People would ask questions such as "If proposition A is true *de fide* (i.e. of the faith) and proposition A implies proposition B, is B true *de fide*, even though the Church may not have yet said so?"! This style of theology was reflected in "manual" theology. Manuals were the set textbooks used in seminaries which spelt out various theses, gave them a theological "note" (or degree of certainty), and then set out to establish them through the use of reason and authority.

These sweeping generalizations are not without their exceptions. Already the seeds of change were being sown. Key figures here are Hans Möhler of the Tübingen school of theology and John Henry Newman, who both sought to make theology more historically minded. Perhaps Newman's late entry into Catholicism allowed him to escape the strictures of the then dominant theology and to thus strike out in a different direction.

Protestant Theology in the Nineteenth Century

The diverse situation in Protestant theology was in marked constrast with the general uniformity found within Catholic theology. Here we find a plurality of theologies which prefigure, in germinal form, the large scale pluralism of the twentieth century.

The beginning of nineteenth century Protestant theology was marked by a great concern with religious feeling. The Pietist movement saw religion as a matter of cultivating profound religious feelings and personal piety. The systematic exposition of this approach can be found in the work of the great theologian, Friedrich Schleiermacher (1768–1834), for whom the starting point of theological reflection is the feeling of absolute dependence. From this starting point Schleiermacher developed a Christology and an ecclesiology, though his trinitarian thought appeared to many to be an awkward addendum to his work. His was a theology grounded in human experience, which proved both its strength and its weakness. Judging this approach too anthropocentric, Swiss theologian Karl Barth later developed his own dialectic theology, a theology of the Word, in reaction to the liberal romanticism of Schleiermacher. The

Pietist theology of religious feeling impacted upon Catholicism in the form of the Modernist movement.

Turning away from the inner world of religious experience, some Protestant theologians began making use of the new critical historical methods developed in studying ancient texts, applying them to the Scriptures. This represented a major shift from seeing the Scriptures as the authoritative word of God to seeing them as historical documents of largely human origin. The Scriptures were examined with the same critical methods used to study other ancient writers. In the late nineteenth century this gave rise to the first "quest for the historical Jesus," which sought to reconstruct the life of Jesus from the diverse accounts found in the Gospels. Many of those involved in the quest saw their historical methods as a way of liberating Jesus from dogmatic accretions. Perhaps the greatest theologian involved in this approach was Adolf von Harnack, who felt that the early dogmas of Christianity were an unwelcome intrusion of Greek philosophy into the pure message of the Gospels.

On the other hand, the end of the nineteenth century witnessed the birth of the modern fundamentalist movement. With their philosophical origins in positivism, fundamentalists rejected the relativization brought about by critical history and accepted a literal interpretation of the Bible as normative for Christian living. The literal truth of the Bible in all matters, from the accounts of creation and fall, to the virginal conception and physical resurrection of Jesus, became the touchstone of orthodoxy. Their conservative theology stood in sharp contrast to the liberal assumptions of the critical historical scholars noted above. Such fundamentalism continues to have a significant impact in North American culture and politics. In a milder version, it can be found in various evangelical approaches to theology and the Bible.

And there were those who were more concerned with the importance of the Gospel message for transforming social conditions. The Social Gospel movement, the Emancipation movement and others developed their own theologies of social action and transformation. In their hands the Gospel became a tool for social criticism which empowered them to challenge the social evils of the day. This movement was stronger in England and North America than in Europe. In many ways it prefigured the later developments in Liberation and Feminist theologies.

Without the strong central authority found in Catholicism, Protestant theology was always going to have more freedom to explore new theological methods and avenues of discovery. In a way this freedom was part of their identity, a continued protest against the impositions of a central ecclesial authority. The resulting plurality of theological styles was inevitable, as new ways of appreciating the diverse reality of faith were uncovered. Equally inevitable was the increasing pressure on Catholic theology, aware of the new insights present in Protestant circles, but restricted by a leadership which was threatened by the implications of those insights.

The Shift from the Nineteenth Century to the Twentieth Century

Historically, the shift from the nineteenth century to the twentieth was very painful for the Catholic Church. Its continued reaction against the modern world gave rise to unbearable tensions, which eventually expressed themselves within the Church. The most notable of these was the Modernist movement, which, as the name implied, sought to modernize Catholicism and its theology. Central to the Modernists' approach was the use of new methods of historical analysis which led to new interpretations of scripture, and an emphasis on personal religious experience. In this they were drawing upon two of the major approaches within Protestant theology.

In their enthusiasm for the new, the Modernists rejected hierarchical religion, ecclesiastical authority and scholastic theology. They sought to establish religious experience, piety and mysticism as central to religious life and theological debate. Their opposition to Church authority and their radical conclusions in interpreting scripture led to a swift response from the Catholic Church. The Holy Office produced a decree, *Lamentabili*, condemning Modernist errors. This was soon followed by an encyclical from Pope Pius X, *Pascendi*, adding papal authority to the condemnation. Teaching positions were lost, careers were ruined, many left the Catholic Church. An internal witch hunt was set up and anyone suspected of deviating from the "party line" was condemned as a Modernist. As often happens with a radical new movement, not only are its answers rejected, but even its questions are suspect. However, the questions the Modernists were asking did not go away, and in many ways contemporary Catholic theology is still responding to the agenda set by the Modernists.

In Protestant theology the shift was more a dialectical development of forces already at work. The liberal romanticism of Schleiermacher elicited a reaction in Barth's theology of the Word. Liberalism and Evangelicalism continued to struggle over the identity of Protestant faith. Fundamentalists and those adopting critical historical method were in regular conflict over the interpretation of the Bible. While the beginning of the twentieth century witnessed a major crisis in Catholicism, Protestant theology continued to be pulled in several different directions.

Now I shall turn to some of the social and cultural forces to which twentieth century theologies were seeking to respond. Indeed, these forces are still shaping our present world in very powerful ways.

The Theory of Evolution

Darwin's theory of evolution put an end to a static view of the universe, a static metaphysics. It is difficult to overestimate the influence that this new view of the world has had. From its humble origins in Darwin's journals, it has now become the dominant metaphor for understanding the universe. Everything is seen in evolutionary terms—life, society, the Church, galaxies, everything! We have moved in the period of one century from being a culture in which change was suspect to one in which change is expected, where lack of change is suspect. This is a significant challenge for the Catholic Church, which had prided itself precisely on the fact that it did not change. It was the others, the Protestants, who changed, and that was a sign of their error! Of course, it is not as if Protestant theology had no difficulty with the theory of evolution. For fundamentalists, rejection of the theory of evolution in light of Biblical accounts of creation and fall remains an indicator of orthodox Christian faith.

Since Darwin, several attempts at a dynamic metaphysics

have been made, e.g. Whitehead's process philosophy, Lonergan's emergent probability, Teilhard de Chardin's evolutionary thought. The specific details of these have not been as significant as the intellectual shift which they symbolize. It should also be said that not all the effects of this change have been positive. Many enthusiasts carried the theory of evolution over into the social sphere to develop the notion of social Darwinism. The survival of the fittest became not simply a biological explanation, but a political program where the "fit" survive and the "unfit," the poor, the invalid, the dispossessed, are left to die for the "improvement" of society. The question of the political consequences of evolutionary thought are raised by the Political Theology of Johann Baptist Metz (see Chapter 11). On the other hand, Karl Rahner has integrated an evolutionary account of creation into his Christological vision of the world (see Chapter 9).

The Shift to the Person

As I have already indicated in the previous chapter, overall, metaphysics has lost the battle (if not the war!) against philosophies of the person. Since Descartes, there has been a shift to the person, to personal categories, from which Catholic theology had been largely "protected." This shift continued in the philosophies of Kant, Hegel, Kierkegaard, existentialism . . . . Overall, philosophical anthropology has replaced metaphysics as a key theological tool.

Indeed, one could argue that this shift was already prefigured in the Reformation. Martin Luther had already attempted to shift the language of theology from metaphysical categories to the categories of personal experience. The resulting clash in theological metaphors and the subsequent Catholic reaction helped to isolate the Catholic Church from subsequent shifts in philosophy. In many ways, Luther was centuries ahead of his time, since even Lutheranism quickly resorted to the metaphysical scholasticism that Luther had rejected as an inadequate description of human experience. The shift to the person is evidenced in the anthropological approach of Rahner and Lonergan, the psychological theology of Sebastian Moore, and the existential exegesis of Rudolph Bultmann.

The Discovery of History

The nineteenth century saw an explosion of critical historical studies, which threw into confusion many dogmatic certainties. Such studies were critical in the sense that they no longer took sources at their face value. Everything, every authority, was subject to the closest scrutiny. A hermeneutics of suspicion had been discovered! In ecclesial circles, this critical historical investigation resulted in dogmas being studied in their historical context, and the condemnation of past figures being called into question—nothing escaped historical examination. A key Catholic figure in this movement was the German historian Doellinger, who eventually left Catholicism after Vatican I's declaration of papal infallibility. Doellinger felt he could not accept it on historical grounds.

This interest in critical history gave rise to the "quest for the historical Jesus," the attempt to use the methods of critical history to uncover the "real" story of Jesus of Nazareth. Numerous 'lives of Jesus' were written, most of which scandalized the faithful, who had accepted the Gospel accounts uncritically as biographical accounts of Jesus' ministry. However, the quest was deemed a failure when Albert Schweitzer (who was later awarded the Nobel Prize for his medical work with lepers in Lambarene, Africa) showed how the various historians had created a Jesus in their own image and likeness. Recently, theology, more aware of the difficulties of the method, has seen renewed interest in the "quest for the historical Jesus."

The discovery of critical history was one of the driving forces of the Modernist movement. While sections of Protestant theology were forging ahead, the Catholic Church found itself ill-equipped to deal with the questions raised by historical studies, locked as it was into ahistorical, static thought forms. Its condemnation of Modernism also led to a suppression of critical history, at least in the area of scriptural studies. It was only in 1942, when Pius XII wrote his encyclical, *Divino Afflante Spiritu*, that Catholic scholars were again allowed access to the methods of critical history, which Protestants had been using for over one hundred years. The impact of these studies is still being felt in Catholic theology and is one of the major sources of conflict at present between it and the magisterium (i.e. the official teaching authority of the Catholic Church). There is hardly a major contemporary theologian whose work has not been affected by the methods of modern critical history.

Another outcome of critical history is that history, as a category, has become important in theology—historicity is now accepted as an essential part of being human.

The Problem of Meaning

One of the key aspects of the discovery of critical history is that it forces us to face the problem of meaning. An uncritical history finds meaning as immediate in the text. One simply has to take a good look to see what is there, as in biblical fundamentalism. A critical history subjects the text to scrutiny. It recognizes the historical context and especially how that context differs from that of the present. It recognizes the gap in the meaning world of the past and that of the present. This raises many difficulties. How can we translate meaning from one meaning world to another? How is meaning passed on from one generation to the next? How do we interpret the past, especially past texts, and remain faithful to their meaning world and ours and to the tradition which bears that text?

Under the pressure of this movement, the linguistic exegesis of the nineteenth century gave way to hermeneutics in the twentieth. In the theological sphere, one outcome of this was that the gap between the carpenter from Galilee and twentieth century humanity became a yawning chasm. How is the life and death of Jesus in an obscure part of the world meaningful to contemporary humankind? Albert Schweitzer discovered to his shock that the Jesus of history was not the mild-mannered preacher of moral virtue, as painted by Schweitzer's contemporaries, but a powerful apocalyptic preacher, convinced of the imminence of the end of the world, a totally alien figure for the early twentieth century. Bridging the gap between now and then has become an important consideration for contemporary theology. There is hardly a major contemporary theologian who is not aware of the issues and concerns raised by hermeneutics.

A Change in the Notion of Culture

Nineteenth century theology was almost entirely a European creation. European culture was The Culture to which all other cultures should aspire. As we have already noted, Benedict XV even spoke of one of the functions of the Church as bringing culture to the barbarians. However, the twentieth century brought an end to that. Not only was Europe torn apart by two world wars, and hence lost any claim to moral superiority, but in general we grew to a richer appreciation of other non-European cultures. Thus, we saw a move from a classicist to an empirical understanding of culture, from culture as normative, to culture as the object of empirical study. I have already spoken of the significance of this in Chapter 1.

Indeed one should not underestimate the impact of two world wars on twentieth century theology. Germany had been, and continues to be, a powerhouse of theological thought. Many German theologians, both Catholic and Protestant, were powerfully affected by the impact of seeing their "high" European culture being drawn into the barbarism of war. Under such circumstances it is difficult to maintain a position of cultural superiority or normativity. The shadow of the Holocaust still falls over the theological landscape.

If I had to find words to express the main characteristics of contemporary theology, I would probably use the following ones. Where I feel they need further explanation over and above what I have already said, I shall add a few explanatory comments.

Critico-Historical—employing the tools of critical history.

Hermeneutic—concerned with questions of meaning and its transmission.

Pluralistic—there is no one style of doing theology. Partly this is the natural outcome of the breakdown in the classicist notion of culture. Partly it is because there is no longer any way of enforcing uniformity on the theological community. Pluralism has allowed for a rich diversity within theology; however, it also can be used to cover over what are really deep divisions.

Suspicious of Authority—contemporary theology has become suspicious of the use of ecclesiastical authority to settle theological debates. There have been too many instances of theologians whose work has been rejected by ecclesiastical authority, only for it to become the new orthodoxy for a new generation. One need only recall that prior to Vatican II, Karl

Rahner was held suspect by Catholic authorities, only to have his theological approach vindicated by the Council. The use of authority is now subject to a hermeneutics of suspicion, the suspicion that what is at stake is not orthodoxy, but the uncritical and unexamined assumptions of those in power.

Anti-metaphysical—this is a further outcome of the suspicion of authority. Metaphysical systems are often seen as standing on nothing but the authority of their creators and the tradition they generate. Kant has left the contemporary world with the suspicion that any metaphysics is either uncritical (in the sense explained in the previous chapter) or meaningless. As I have said above, metaphysics has been largely replaced by philosophies of the human person.

Scriptural—with the encyclical *Divino Afflante Spiritu*, Catholic theology has become increasingly scripturally based, something which has always been a feature of Protestant theology. Scripture is no longer used as a source of proof texts, but as a wellspring of themes and inspiration for theology. There is renewed interest in the "historical Jesus" and the history of the apostolic Church. These have provided rich matter for theological reflection.

Personalist—as I have already indicated, contemporary theology draws heavily on philosophical anthropology. This has been richly complemented by insights from human psychology, especially the depth psychologies of Freud and Jung, and from existentialist and personalist philosophies such as those of Martin Buber. The categories of theology are now drawn much more from human experience, from interpersonal relationships.

Dialectical—theology has developed the maturity to recognize its own pluralism. Of itself, this pluralism raises questions of a theological nature. How are these diverse theologies related? How can we identify and overcome divergences between pluriform theologies? This is a dialectic process of identifying strengths and weaknesses, of finding complementarities and oppositions, of seeking a more comprehensive picture.

Seeking Foundations—appreciation for dialectic leads to a search for foundations, a quest for methodology. While we can recognize diversity and plurality within theology, we still recognize each different theology as theology! What is it then that grounds this unity of identity within a diversity of expression? What makes theology theology? Here I may quote Peter Chirico from his work *Infallibility*, where he states:

> Pluralism is inevitable in the present condition. . . . Yet pluralism must not be viewed as an end in itself; rather it is a stage towards the richness of eschatological unity. This means that all meanings or actualizations of human potential are ultimately shareable and hence universal, but not now (p.319).

The search for foundations is the first step towards achieving that unity.

Conclusion

If I had to nominate one area as a central problem for contemporary theology, I would have to say that it is the whole area of dogma. Much of contemporary theology has taken to its heart the Enlightenment criticism of dogma, or it has declared the hermeneutic problems associated with dogma to be insurmountable. Contemporary theology is struggling to find a place for dogma, to grasp its significance and meaning, both for theology and for the Churches as a whole. Can dogma survive in the face of critical history, of hermeneutics and a suspicion of authority?

My own position is that it can and must, though only on the basis of a critical appropriation of the past. Though this is not the time or place for a defence of this position, the role of dogma will be one of the themes which I shall trace through the various authors that we shall be considering.

DISCUSSION QUESTIONS

• It could be argued that for much of the twentieth-century Catholic theology was simply catching up with Protestant theology. Would you agree?

• How do you think that the theological developments of the last one hundred years have affected Church practice and life?

CHAPTER 4

Method in Theology

Having looked at the differences between past and contemporary theology it is now time to consider the question of methodology—what is a theologian doing when he or she is doing theology? As I noted in the previous chapter, methodological questions are foundational for theology and, as such, are a matter for current concern and debate among theologians. Since this is a matter of current debate, I cannot hope to put forward some definite conclusion as to the present consensus, since there is none. I do hope, however, to put forward a position which I believe may help the newcomer, looking in for the first time, to gain some insight into the variety to be found within contemporary theology.

I have raised methodological questions in the chapter on the nature of theology—for example, how does theology differ from science and philosophy? One answer to this question may be to say that theology involves a systematic study of revelation. This distinguishes it from science, which studies empirical data, and philosophy, which starts from human reason. However, it also raises many more questions, such as what do we mean when we say something is revealed? What does it mean to say, for instance, that the ten commandments were revealed by God to Moses, or that the divinity of Jesus is revealed, or the infallibility of the Pope? And most importantly, how do we verify such a claim? Scripture? Tradition? Present teaching authority?

Clearly some concept of revelation is a central starting point for theology. Moreover, as we shall see, the way in which we conceive of revelation will affect the way in which we do theology. If we conceive of revelation as the imparting of divine truths in propositional form, this will have a big influence on the style of our theology—indeed we may end up doing theology in the manner of the nineteenth century manuals.

The other thing that needs to be said is that one's conception of revelation is never "politically neutral." To claim the authority of divine revelation is a political act, at least within a religious community such as a church. It establishes a power relationship between the bearer and the receiver of revelation. This is most clearly instanced in theocratic states such as Iran. Within secular states, such a power relationship is restricted to being mainly within Christian communities. To speak of revelation is to locate a focus of authority, and hence of power, within a church. Such power has frequently been misused and hence is subject to suspicion. However, the claims to divine authority will continue to be of significance for the Churches for the majority of people. This makes a contemporary understanding of revelation a matter of urgency for the Churches, though one fraught with political difficulties.

As a first entry point into the notion of revelation, I would like to draw on the work of Avery Dulles. In his book, *Models of Revelation*, Dulles discusses six models of revelation which he finds operative in contemporary theology. While I do not agree with every aspect of Dulles' analysis, I do find it helpful in that it highlights the various issues and concerns which need to be addressed in any account of revelation.

1. Revelation as Doctrine

Here revelation is conceived in terms of "clear propositional statements attributed to God." Such propositions are to be found in the Bible (especially for evangelical Christians) and in the pronouncements of the Church magisterium (for Catholics). Such statements are direct verbal communication from God (or at least should be treated as such). Aspects of this position are reflected in Vatican I, which speaks of the written and unwritten traditions of the New Testament coming "from the mouth of Christ himself" or by "dictation from the Holy Spirit." The most extreme form is found in fundamentalism.

One difficulty of this model is that it fails to come to grips with the question of meaning. Propositions are fixed, but, as cultures change, the meaning given to propositions will vary.

How can we ensure that meanings are preserved within changing cultures if we have canonized past formalized propositions? Inasmuch as this model fails to address such questions of meaning, one would have to say that it is hermeneutically naive.

2. Revelation as History

Here, revelation is conceived in terms of God's mighty deeds, especially those recorded in the Bible, e.g. Exodus, and especially the resurrection of Jesus. Revelation is claimed not to be propositional but to be historical. Thus, revelation is never closed until the eschatological completion of history, when the true meaning of history will be clear. In the meantime, the resurrection of Jesus is a foretaste of that eschatological completion. The main proponent of such an approach is Protestant theologian, Wolfhart Pannenberg. Even Vatican II speaks of God's revelation in word *and deed*.

One weakness of this approach is the neglect of the word aspect of revelation, i.e. the interpretative word of the prophet which speaks God's intent in history. While this model helped introduce history into our concept of revelation (especially in the light of our earlier comments on the importance of history as a category in theology), it failed to recognize the ambiguity of history and the necessity of an interpretative word to express the meaning of history within that ambiguity.

3. Revelation as Inner Experience

Here revelation is conceived in terms of mystical experience, as "privileged interior experience of grace or communion with God" (Dulles, p.27). In this model the paradigm of revelation is the mystic in his or her cell. Again, nothing "objective" is said to be revealed, certainly no revealed doctrines. What the mystic experiences is God, and God cannot be reduced to any mere doctrine or definition. Any expression which arises out of the experience is secondary and is meant simply to be a means into the original experience.

In this model, the comments above about the political nature of revelation have some context. When revelation is conceived in terms of inner experience, there is a radical decentering of authority within the community. Anyone can be the subject of a mystical experience. Anyone can be the locus of authority. An ecclesial expression of this would be the Quakers. This model was also part of the Modernist movement and was clearly an aspect which was seen to threaten Catholic Church authority.

Strangely enough, however, the main weakness of this model is that it is prone to elitism. While in theory anyone can be the subject of mystical experience, few are. Most of us are left with so-called secondary formulations. Such secondary formulations may often reflect diametrically opposed positions within different religious traditions. For example, Christian mystical experience is interpreted in theistic terms, i.e. as experience of God, while Buddhist mystical experience may well be interpreted in non-theistic or a-theistic terms. Revelation can become an individualistic and privatized phenomenon. In this way the model fails to come to grips with the social dimension of revelation, that revelation establishes a community held together by common meanings and values.

4. Revelation as Dialectic Presence

This is the most difficult of the models that Dulles presents. Its main exponent is the leading Protestant theologian, Karl Barth, though many say that Barth has his Catholic counterpart in Hans Urs von Balthasar. In this model "God encounters the human subject when it pleases him by means of a word in which faith recognizes him to be present" (Dulles, p.28). This word "simultaneously reveals and conceals the divine presence" (ibid.), since even in revelation God remains transcendent and wholly other. The model thrives on such paradoxes.

The main strength of the model is that it is explicitly Trinitarian. In revelation God speaks God's Word, which cannot be distinguished from God—God's Word is God. Further, the Spirit enables us to receive God's Word as God's Word, without reducing it to a merely human word. For Barth, it is very important that we do not place ourselves in the position of judging God, since it is God who judges us. All we can do is accept God's revelation in faith. As such, it acted as an important corrective to the liberal Protestantism of the nineteenth century, which was in danger of falling over into a mere humanism.

However, there was also a negative side to this position. As an extreme stance, its end result is fideism, i.e. faith without any ground other than the divine authority, without any reference to human reason. One must simply accept the claim to divine authority without question. It is of no matter that what is being believed may be absurd. As we have already noted, Barth will eventually claim, echoing Tertullian, an early Father of the Church, "Because it is absurd, I believe"!

5. Revelation as New Awareness

In this model, revelation is conceived in terms of a change in the subjectivity of the human person, brought about by grace (faith) which enables him or her to see things in a new light. Again, in this model nothing "objective" is revealed, no revealed truth. All that occurs is that a new conscious state is brought about, which enables people to grasp what is already there to be grasped if they had not been blinded by their own bias and sin. The paradigm of this model is the prophet, who, in the light of his or her transformed consciousness, sees the suffering of the poor as the result of social injustice. The fact of suffering is always there to be seen, but it is only in the light of consciousness transforming grace that the real meaning is grasped.

The strength of this model is that, of all the models, it takes seriously the Kantian question of the role of the subject in the constitution or creation of knowledge. The subject does not passively receive knowledge or revelation. It is rather the coming together of subject and object, an act in which the subject plays an active role of uncovering meaning. However, the model also underplays the "objective" side of revelation since it denies that there is any revealed "object." While this may be appealing to some, it does come up against traditional concerns about the centrality of Jesus, of scripture, of Church dogmas.

6. Revelation as Symbolic Mediation

Dulles recognizes the shortcomings of these various models and so seeks to overcome them by developing what is, in fact, a further model, that of symbolic mediation. Dulles sees this model as providing a "dialectic retrieval" of the positive values of the other models, so that this new model will "sublate" the others. He considers this as a more fruitful approach than either adopting one, eclectically picking bits and pieces from each, or providing a false harmonization.

Dulles' starting point for the model of symbolic mediation is that revelation never occurs in some purely interior experience of God. It is always mediated through a symbol—that is to say, through an external sign that works mysteriously on human consciousness. Such symbols suggest far more than can be clearly described or defined. Revelatory symbols are those which express and mediate God's self-communication. A paradigm example could be the crucifixion, which invites us to explore the mystery of divine justice. As a symbol it expresses far more than can be put into words.

However, he acknowledges difficulties with his model. He is aware that it might lead to problems such as "subjectivism, relativism and a reductionist humanism." While he tries to maintain that Christian symbols are not infinitely pliable with regard to their interpretation, the question remains open as to just how pliable they are. Dulles sought to overcome this pliability by giving doctrine a role in interpreting revelatory symbols. Yet this just begs the question as one is left asking where these doctrines come from in the first place, if not by symbolic mediation.

As an overall comment, we might notice that these different models swing between a focus on the "object" and the "subject" of revelation. They also display different understandings of the relationship between subject and object within revelation. I would say that many of these differences reveal different philosophical assumptions. The differences are not strictly "theological" but come about from different conceptions of knowledge, reality and the relationship between these.

Secondly, we can also note that each particular model of revelation will give rise to a different theological method. The revelation as doctrine model will give rise to a theological positivism with a focus on logic and a concurrent neglect of history. The revelation as history model will take its stand on critico-historical method. Revelation as inner experience will focus on mystical theology. Revelation as dialectic presence will rely heavily on a paradoxical method. Revelation as new awareness will develop a praxis-oriented methodology, i.e. one concerned with committed social action. Finally, revelation as symbolic mediation leads to a hermeneutic approach to theology. These various approaches to revelation can thus be seen to be the source of much of the theological pluralism in the current theological situation.

Finally, we should note that the various models also tend to have a different "directionality," either from above down, or from below up. Revelation may be seen as God's irruption into the human situation with the voice of authority (a voice from the clouds), as in the revelation as doctrine model or the dialectic model. Alternatively, it may be seen as arising out of the human situation, from "below," as in the inner experience or the new–awareness model with their focus on the experience of the human person.

It is here that we come up against the basic dilemma which revelation poses. The basic problem, and indeed the suspicion, with regard to any claim to revelation, is how am I to recognize that what is being "revealed" in fact comes from God and is not simply an attempt to gain some power over me? Many religions and persons claim to be bearers of revelation, often making contradictory claims. How can I distinguish between them? Moreover, if I have to make such a judgment, am I not placed in the difficult position of having to "judge" God rather than being "judged by God"? Basically we have returned to the question of the relationship between faith and reason—how can I determine reasonable *a priori* principles for recognizing the word of God as the word of God, without reducing it in the process to a merely human word and robbing it of its power and authority?

A simple way of stating this problem is to ask: "Is something revealed because it is experienced as bringing salvation, or does it bring salvation because it is revealed?" If something comes to me with a claim to being revealed, yet I experience it as oppressive and life-denying, can I take its claim seriously? On the other hand, if I experience something as liberating and life-affirming, does this necessarily mean that it comes as a revelation from God? Is it not possible that my judgments as to what is oppressive or liberating, life-denying or life-affirming, may also be distorted?

Theologically, this gives rise to a dialectic situation. Firstly, you must stand over your theological sources, see them in their human origins, criticize them, reconstruct them, analyze them in the finest detail, in the light of the authority of your own experience of human existence and faith commitment. You must exclude no evidence, allow every question, investigate every hypothesis, consider every deduction. Reason must be allowed its full rights of investigation. Anything less than this will in the final analysis fall over into fideism.

However, that is not the end of the story. For, secondly and just as importantly, you must stand under your theological sources and allow them to criticize you, to see you in your human origins, to reconstruct you and analyze you in the finest detail, in the light of their own claim to authority. You must exclude no possibility of personal bias, of sin which could hinder the truth from coming to light. God's grace must be allowed its full power to transform the theologian. Anything less than this will, in the final analysis, be an arrogance of the intellect.

In the light of this discussion I would propose that we consider revelation in the following terms. Revelation is a hermeneutic process, i.e. a process for the uncovering and transmission of meanings and values which arise in relation to the life, death and resurrection of Jesus of Nazareth. Primarily, these meanings and values are the meaning and value of the person of Jesus himself and the meanings and values he passes on to his disciples. The further process of recovering and transmitting those meanings and values is then carried on under the inspiration of the Holy Spirit. Thus, relevation is God's self-communication in Word and Spirit.

This understanding of revelation should not be seen as restricting revelation to the Christian experience. Other cultures, other peoples may experience the revelation of God. They may uncover meanings and values totally consistent with those found in Christian revelation. However, it does take a normative stance, that Jesus is THE revelation of God so that other revelatory experiences find their true meaning and fulfillment in him.

By considering revelation as a hermeneutic process, I hope that it is possible to do justice to both the movement from below and from above that we saw was part of the models considered previously. It also, I hope, does away with any simple-minded, naive understanding of revelation which fails to come to grips with the full complexity of the reality of revelation.

This notion of revelation as a hermeneutic process, I believe, lies behind the work of Bernard Lonergan in his book *Method in Theology*. Lonergan is a major writer in the area of theological method and we shall be considering some of his contribution later. Here we shall simply consider the final results of his researches on theological method. While Lonergan is concerned with theological method, it is not too difficult to see how his method correlates with an understanding of revelation as a hermeneutic process.

Lonergan has posited eight functional specialties (areas dominated by specific questions, concerns and criteria) within theology, which together constitute a theological method. Such a theological method is not a set of rules which anyone may follow and achieve significant results. It simply delineates what are the stages in the creative, faith-filled process, which moves from data to final results, that constitutes theology. These stages correlate with the stages involved in the process of uncovering and transmitting meanings and values. While Lonergan gives a critical grounding for these stages, we shall simply note them and their relationships.

1. Research

The first area is simply a matter of attending to the data, be it scriptural texts, Church documents, history, human experience. No data can *a priori* be excluded, though clearly there will be a focus on the human world of meaning and value rather than the empirical data of the natural sciences. Even within our human world of meanings and values, some data will be more significant than others—the text of scripture will be of more interest than data on grain sales in ancient Rome!

In this specialty one attempts to precisely determine which data is accurate, correct. For example, scholars expend great effort in determining what is the exact text of the New Testament. All we have is a variety of manuscripts dating from the third and fourth centuries (and, of course, later periods). These manuscripts often differ due to transcription errors. The scholarly task is to attempt a reconstruction of the original text.

Similar problems arise with other historical data, such as various Church documents throughout the ages.

2. Interpretation

Accurate texts and data are one thing, meaning is another. Having gathered the data, what does it mean? How do we interpret it? This is the level of exegesis, of historical contextualization. When dealing with scriptural texts, the scholar requires a detailed knowledge of the literature of the era, of the ancient languages. In recent times, light has been shed on the interpretation of scripture by the discovery of the Dead Sea Scrolls, which have provided a mass of literature written around New Testament times. This literature has filled out the historical context of New Testament literature enormously. Interpretation of this type is a difficult, scholarly task, not an area for beginners.

However, the specialty, interpretation, should not be seen as restricted to literature or artifacts from the past. Interpretation can just as much be about present events. When dealing, for example, with personal experience, knowledge of psychology is a similar essential. In other matters one may need to draw on sociology or economics to provide a fuller interpretation. In any act of interpretation it is important to remember that all data has a context which shapes its meaning, and any interpretative task must take into account that context in all its dimensions.

3. History

Having gathered the possible, probable and likely meanings of the basic data, one then seeks to determine what is moving forward, what the historical movements are, the progress or decline, which the meanings represent. Meanings form patterns, patterns reveal not only the individual intent of a particular person, but a school of thought, an historical movement. Connections are made between persons, between movements, between events. Often these connections may not be known by those caught up in the events themselves. The people themselves may not know what is moving forward. However the historian's task is to construct a meaningful narrative. In this

way the past, either personal, cultural or religious, is recon-
structed out of the multiplicity of meanings uncovered through
interpretation.

4. Dialectics

In general, our experience of theology, and the human sciences
as a whole, indicates that the results of this process will not be
universally accepted. There will be a variety of different interpretations and historical judgments all drawing on the same
data. Some such interpretations and judgments may be complementary. However, they may also be contradictory. Where
one applauds progress, another condemns decline; where one
grasps truth, another uncovers lies. It is this difficulty which
makes dialectics necessary. Dialectics seeks to uncover the bases
for these contradictions, not in the data, but in the subjects who
interpret the data. Different subjects come to the data with different commitments, different value stances, different philosophies. Without at this stage judging between them, dialectics
clarifies the various value stances and the interpretations they
give rise to. Dialectics takes the Kantian critique of knowledge
seriously in that it makes explicit the subject's role in constitut-
ing knowledge.

These four stages constitute the movement "from below" in
Lonergan's method. They delineate the stages of the upward
movement of human creativity, what is classically referred to
as "reason," though they also take into account values (note
that the relationship between reason and values is a disputed
area!). Lonergan would claim that a faith commitment of itself
is not essential to this upward movement. As such, these four
stages could equally be part of religious studies as of theology.
They are part of a common academic commitment.

For Lonergan, however, at the peak of this process stands
conversion, which calls for a faith commitment, a change of
heart and a gift of grace, to take a stand in the face of the
conflicting positions uncovered by dialectics. Lonergan identifies three basic conversions: religious, moral, and intellectual.
Others add psychic.

Religious conversion entails a "falling in love without
restriction," "being gripped by ultimate concern" (cf. Paul
Tillich). It arises out of the gift of God's love poured into our

hearts by the Holy Spirit (Romans 5:5). For the Christian, such conversion is mediated by the life, death and resurrection of Jesus, who is the Father's Word of unconditional love incarnated in human history.

Moral conversion entails the recognition of personal moral responsibility, that it is through one's moral decision-making that one makes oneself who one is. Such a conversion is "good news and bad news." The bad news is the responsibility for sin and failure in one's life. The good news is that there is a way out, through the exercise of personal responsibility under the grip of God's grace. Moral conversion brings about a hope for change, both personally and historically.

Intellectual conversion entails the recognition of the link between understanding and reality. It implies a rejection of the Kantian opposition between meaning (interpretation) and reality. Rather it understands that reality is intrinsically meaningful and that truth is arrived at through correct interpretation. Intellectual conversion rejects any opposition between subjectivity and objectivity, but sees "genuine objectivity as the fruit of authentic subjectivity." In my experience, the presence or absence of intellectual conversion is a source of much theological disagreement. Indeed, many of the differences in the various models of revelation considered by Dulles arise from problems associated with intellectual conversion.

Finally, psychic conversion entails a personal appropriation of the role of symbol, of dream, of beauty within the ongoing drama of life, of history, of culture. It acknowledges the role of psychic forces at work within subjects, structuring their experience, shaping the expression of meaning and values in life. Psychic conversion raises questions about how we attend to data, about data, especially in our personal lives, that we simply refuse to see. It also raises questions about the creative process whereby we seek to communicate our insights to others in word and symbol.

In this context, it is important to realize that the faith which arises out of conversion is not opposed to reason. It does not impose limits on what question can be asked, or even determine *a priori* what answers should be given. Rather, conversion involves the transformation of the subject, and so allows the full dynamics of reason to be operative. As Lonergan argues, faith is not a leap into irrationality, but a leap into reason, away from the irrationality of sin and bias, in all its forms, both personal and social.

We shall now consider the final four functional specialties which constitute the downward dynamic of theology.

5. Foundations

The task of foundations is the objectification of conversion. Foundations will analyze the cause of diversity within dialectics on the basis of the presence or absence of conversion. While dialectics simply notes the diversity, foundations will take a stand, identifying the presence or absence of conversion through the judgments that have been made. For Lonergan, it is the converted subject who is the foundational reality for theology. Whatever sources the theologian may draw upon—scripture, human experience, what have you—it will be the presence or absence of conversion which will determine the type of theology that is produced.

Further, foundations will seek the proper categories to express conversion and the symbols which can mediate the process of conversion. Such categories may be general, in that they apply to a broad range of human sciences, as well as theology (for example, culture); or they may be special in that they apply specifically to a religious reality (for example, grace or sin). We shall see examples of such foundational theology in the works of Rahner, Moore and Metz.

6. Doctrines

Out of foundations come doctrines. Foundations will focus on the converted subject, doctrines on the judgments which flow from that conversion. Materially, these judgments can be found among those analyzed in history and dialectics. However, now is the time for taking a stand, for committing oneself to concrete, particular judgments which are central to the life of the converted subject.

In an age suspicious of dogma, one may ask if such a stage is in any way essential. Why do we need to be so definitive? Why not allow for a "legitimate pluralism"? Firstly, we should note that historically such judgments have been made, in, for example, Church Councils such as Nicea and Chalcedon, and so we need to ask what such judgments mean. It seems clear to me that the purpose of those making such judgments was to settle definitively controverted and community-splitting issues. Were they mistaken, not just in their particular judgments but also in their sense that such definitive judgments needed to be made? Can we simply relegate such judgments into the basket of "historical and cultural conditioning" without recognizing any further claim on our faith?

Secondly, we need to realize that this is not simply an ecclesial problem. There are not only ecclesial doctrines but also social ones. The debate over nuclear arms is an example of dialectically opposed judgments where each side, pro- or anti-disarmament, has taken a definitive stance, made a particular opposed judgment. In such cases, do we say that we should allow for a "legitimate pluralism," even though, as some would claim, we are putting the future of the human race at risk?

7. Systematics

The task of systematics is to give systematic expression to what has been stated in doctrines. Systematics will seek to develop appropriate systems of conceptualization, often drawing on the resources of philosophy and other disciplines, to place the various doctrines within a framework of thought, relating one to the other, sorting out apparent inconsistencies arising from different cultural expressions and historical contexts. Systematics comes closest to Anselm's definition of theology as faith seeking understanding. Especially in areas of faith where one is dealing with the mystery that is God, often such understanding can only be analogous. This finds expression in the classical psychological analogies of the Trinity in Augustine and Aquinas.

8. Communication

The final theological task, communication, is concerned with the "external" relations of theology to the culture. It is not good enough for theologians simply to formulate great understandings; they must also deliver the goods in a way that people understand! Communication involves a sensitivity to the culture, the thought forms, the symbols of those whom theology addresses. Finally, with communications a hermeneutic circle is complete, since what is communicated then becomes the data for a new round, in future generations, of research, interpretation, history, dialectics and so on.

Conclusion

Lonergan's method is based on the "transcendental imperatives"—be attentive, be intelligent, be reasonable, be responsible and be in love (transcendental in the Kantian sense, i.e. *a priori* structures within the subject). These imperatives correlate with the basic conversions—be attentive with psychic conversion; be intelligent, be reasonable with intellectual; be responsible with moral; be in love with religious. They further correlate with the functional specialties—be attentive with research and communications; be intelligent with interpretation and systematics; be reasonable with history and doctrines; be responsible with dialectics and foundations; be in love with religious conversion, which arches over the whole process.

As I have argued, this method in theology correlates with a notion of revelation as hermeneutic process, the uncovering and transmission of meanings and values arising from the life, death and resurrection of Jesus. At the peak of Lonergan's process is the fully authentic, fully converted subject, Jesus Christ, a man like us in all things but sin, who not only speaks God's word, but is God's Word, who not only reveals God's will, but is the revelation of God, the revealed revealer. Both revelation and theology find their focus in him.

Historically, the Churches have been very strong on the task of transmission of the meanings and values arising out of Jesus' mission. In the Protestant Churches these meanings and values were seen as revealed definitively in the Bible. In the Catholic Church, the Bible was part of a larger Tradition which was seen as a deposit, something firmly "in possession," which simply needed to be handed on to each new generation. It was, as Fred Crowe has noted, an era of "simple possession of the truth." Hermeneutics, however, has made us aware that in order to hand on truth it must first be uncovered. Truth is not handed on like an inheritance, but is incarnated in minds, hearts and actions. The task of making the truth explicit is a task of uncovering latent and implicit meanings in those minds and hearts and actions so that future generations may make the truth their own. It is this task which requires the ongoing inspiration of the Holy Spirit, prompting us to ever deeper conversion, so that God's Word in Jesus may be heard in all generations and in all cultures.

It is important to note that any particular theological work may cut across many of these specialties. The various tasks are clearly intermeshed, dealing with the same subject matter but with a different thrust. The main point in introducing these various functional specialties is as a way of clarifying what it is that the various theologians we shall be considering are doing. Often theologians are criticized because they did not do this or that, because they fail to live up to criteria and expectations set by someone else. We must approach each theologian on his or her own terms, according to his or her own criteria. The functional specialties will help us clarify some of the limits of the task a theologian may have set for him or herself and so prevent premature and unfair criticism.

DISCUSSION QUESTIONS

- How does one's understanding of revelation affect the way one does theology?

- Give examples of ways in which the meanings and values of the Christian faith are handed on from one generation to the next.

- What role do you give to defined doctrines in the process of revelation?

Bibliography

For the philosophical material in Chapter 2, the reader may like to refer to the fuller accounts in *A History of Philosophy*, Vols 1–9, by Frederick Copleston, New York: Image Books, 1964.

For an indication of the growing significance of sociology in theological thought, see:

G. Baum, *Religion and Alienation*, New York: Paulist Press, 1975.

The theological material in Chapters 1, 3 and 4 constitutes a minicourse in fundamental theology. Here there is much material of high quality:

A. Dulles, *Models of Revelation*, Maryknoll, N.Y.: Orbis Books, 1992; Dublin: Gill and Macmillan, 1983.

G. O'Collins, *Fundamental Theology*, New York: Paulist Press, 1981.

F. Crowe, *Theology of the Christian Word*, New York: Paulist Press, 1987.

R. Latourelle and G. O'Collins (Eds), *Problems and Perspectives of Fundamental Theology*, New York: Paulist Press, 1982.

R. Haight, *The Dynamics of Theology*, New York: Paulist Press, 1990.

F. Fiorenza, *Foundational Theology*, New York: Crossroad, 1985.

For an excellent analysis of the problems of interpretation see:

P. Chirico, *Infallibility* (especially Chapter 1), Wilmington: Michael Glazier, 1983.

For an exploration of the development of Protestant theology see:

A. McGrath, *The Making of Modern German Christology 1750-1990*, Grand Rapids: Apollos, 1994.

For an application of the first three functional specialties to the Scriptures, see:

B. Meyer, *Reality and Illusion in New Testament Scholarship*, Collegeville: Michael Glazier, 1994.

The thought of Bernard Lonergan has been an undeniable influence on the author. The reader may refer to the following:

B. Lonergan, *Method in Theology*, New York: Seabury Press, 1972; London: Darton, Longman and Todd, 1974. *A Second Collection*, Philadelphia/London: Westminster Press/Darton, Longman and Todd, 1974.

PART B

The *Who* of Theology

In this part of the book we shall consider the work of several leading theologians. The aim is not to give a detailed analysis of the work of each, nor even a detailed analysis of a major work of each. My aim is simply to take a major work of each theologian and look at aspects of that work which I feel give the reader some insight into the workings of contemporary theology.

I have provided some background on each author and some historical asides and comments of my own which I hope I have clearly distinguished from descriptive material of the theologian concerned. I have also attempted to illuminate the theological method of each author in the light of the discussion in Chapter 4.

Hopefully the reader will then be able to approach the authors concerned with some confidence of what is going on in contemporary theology and so get more out of their reading.

CHAPTER 5

Hans Küng, *Making Theology Contemporary*

It is fitting that an investigation of contemporary theology should begin with the figure of Hans Küng. Few theologians have been as successful in bringing the insights of modern theological research to a popular audience. Küng's books, particularly his work, *On Being A Christian*, which is still being reprinted after first appearing in 1976, have been big sellers. Their popularity lies not only in their "readability," a rarity with theological works, but also in Küng's willingness to address controversial topics. In this way, he is able to give people the freedom to ask questions without the fear of appearing foolish or of being censured by religious authoritarianism.

Küng first came to theological prominence with his major study, entitled *Justification*, on the work of the leading Protestant theologian, Karl Barth. Here Küng attempts to compare Barth's theology on justification with the position of the Catholic Church. In its published form the work contains two letters, one from Karl Barth, the other from Karl Rahner. The letter from Barth acknowledges the accuracy with which Küng has presented Barth's position on justification. The letter from Rahner states his opinion that Küng has accurately presented the Catholic position on justification. Küng's thesis that the two positions are basically the same represents a major ecumenical achievement, given that the problem of justification has been at the heart of Protestant-Catholic division.

This ecumenical concern brought forth two major works on the Church, *Structures of the Church* and *The Church* and his later study on infallibility, *Infallible?*. His early concern with ecumenical questions brought him to the attention of John XXIII, who invited Küng to attend Vatican II as a theological adviser. His later work on infallibility, brought out after *Humanae Vitae* (1968), caused much consternation among the hierarchy. It has generally been agreed that the book *Infallible?* was poorly written and researched. Basically, Küng argued that *Humanae Vitae* was an example of the exercise of papal infallibility and that *Humanae Vitae* is wrong, therefore infallibility is a false doctrine. However, only the most conservative of theologians have ever argued that *Humanae Vitae* involved the exercise of papal infallibility. Küng did not retract, and after lengthy proceedings with Roman authorities he had his license to teach theology revoked, though he remains a Catholic priest.

Since this work he has written several major works including *On Being a Christian*, *Does God Exist?* and *Eternal Life*.

Material under consideration—*On Being a Christian*, New York/London: Doubleday/Collins, 1976

The work, *On Being a Christian* is in a sense a personal *Summa* of the Christian faith, written from the perspective of contemporary culture and recent biblical and historical research. Yet it is more than just a personal statement. Küng sees his own quest as indicative of the situation of contemporary humanity. Thus it is a book written for those:

> . . . who do not believe, but nevertheless seriously inquire;
> who did believe, but are not satisfied with their unbelief;
> who do believe, but feel insecure in their faith;
> who are at a loss, between belief and unbelief;
> who are skeptical, both about their convictions and about their doubts (p.19).

It is a book for those on the fringes, perhaps the majority of those who have some, if only feeble, alliance with Christianity, who are unable to take their faith unquestioningly.

For these people, Küng is seeking to justify Christianity. However, such a justification cannot be achieved in the abstract way of traditional triumphalist apologetics, arguing from miracles to the divinity of Christ to the role of the Church. For Küng, Christianity is to be justified by looking at the concrete situation of our contemporary world—what are the alternatives? Buddhism, Hinduism, Islam, Marxism, various social movements? What do they have to offer, what are their strengths and weaknesses? How does Christianity compare? How is Christianity challenged and how does it in its turn challenge these alternatives? What is special about Christianity?

The clear answer to this last question is that what is special about Christianity is Jesus Christ. Yet which Christ? The Christ of dogma, of piety, of the fundamentalist? How are we to know that the object of our belief is the Jesus who lived and died in Palestine and not simply a projection, a wish fulfillment, a fantasy of our own making? To answer this question, Küng places great trust in the contemporary advances in critico-historical methods, in modern biblical criticism:

> Because of the work of so many generations of exegetes and the results of the historical-critical method, we are able today to know better than perhaps any former generations of Christians—except the first—the true, original Jesus of history (p.161).

Of course faith is possible without the use of critico-historical methods, but it will always run the risk of naivete, of making Jesus what we want him to be, rather than what he was and is.

In his analysis of the historical Jesus, Küng makes various comparisons between Jesus and four main groupings within Jewish society at the time of Jesus. Thus he variously compares Jesus with the Sadducees, the Zealots, the Essenes and the Pharisees.

For Küng, the Sadducees are those who represented the alliance between religious and political power, those who used religion and politics in order to maintain the status quo and their own position within the status quo. But Jesus was not one of them, not a priest, not a power broker.

The Zealots, on the other hand, are those who sought to overturn the status quo through a violent revolution. They longed for a messiah who would lead them to military victory over the Roman occupiers and establish a theocratic kingdom of God through revolutionary means. But Jesus was not one of them; he came as the messiah of the poor and powerless, riding on a donkey.

The Essenes sought to escape the world by retreating into the desert, setting up a community of the pure, the saved, leaving the world to its own religious and political corruption. Through their monastic lifestyles, their mysticism and rituals, they hoped to create a perfect community and hence establish the kingdom of God. But Jesus was not one of them. Rather than reject the impure, the outcasts, as did the Essenes, he sought them out and claimed that it was to these that the kingdom of God belonged.

The Pharisees, finally, represented the way of "cheerful inconsistency, legal harmonization, diplomatic adjustment and moral compromise" (p.202). These were the separated ones, not in the radical manner of the Essenes, but those whose devotion to the minutiae of the Law placed them, at least in their own eyes, above the uneducated, the public sinners, the poor. However, they did not carry their devotion to the point of complete separation but were willing to compromise, to be in the world but apart, through their adherence to the Law. But Jesus was not one of them. His saying—the Sabbath was made for man, not man for the Sabbath—was offensive to legalistic minds.

Needless to say, Küng sees many parallels between the time of Jesus and our own time, with many of the same tensions, the same "solutions" to the question of leading a "religious" life, being offered today. Behind Küng's description of the Sadducees, it is not hard to see Küng's reaction to a conservative Roman hierarchy and their official theology; behind the Zealots a contemporary "theology of revolution"; behind the Essenes those who choose a "religious" monastic lifestyle; behind the Pharisees, the religiously self-righteous of every age.

Küng's positive analysis of Jesus and the meaning of his life, death and resurrection, leading into the formation of the early Church, is quite lengthy, nearly three hundred pages. I do not intend to go into detail about the contents of these pages, but merely indicate that they touch on just about every area of

Jesus' life and the faith that it gave rise to. Most questions, especially the controversial ones, get a mention, in the light of modern biblical criticism.

Many might find some of Küng's statements a bit scandalous, though generally this is more a function of widespread biblical fundamentalism than any real "offence to faith." On the other hand, one gets the impression that Küng at times sets out to shock, to say something that will deliberately upset those of a conservative mold. As I have said above, Küng is attracted to controversy.

For the purpose of this study, I shall concentrate on Küng's handling of miracles. Küng's starting point is that the notion of miracle is problematic to a modern scientific culture. For the Church and its proclamation of the Gospel, the miracles of Jesus have become an embarrassment, something which happened "in olden days" but which are simply not part of our own human experience. In his analysis of the miracle stories of Jesus, Küng tries to find a path between a fundamentalist, uncritical acceptance of all the miracle stories of Jesus and a rationalist scepticism which simply sees miracles as impossible, following the rationalist critique of miracles by David Hume.

The basic problem for contemporary culture, as Küng sees it, is "whether the miracles ascribed to Jesus, which, as far as the text is concerned, were contrary to the laws of nature, were historical facts" (p.227). Modern biblical criticism has shown that the miracle stories within the Gospels are as deeply ingrained within the Jesus tradition as is his preaching activity. It would be dishonest to simply pass over them in an embarrassed silence. On the other hand, a critical spirit requires that they not be accepted just at face value. Biblical criticism also makes clear that the miracle stories contain elements of embellishment and legendary accretions which mean they are not merely accounts of "what happened."

But the question remains—what really happened? In asking such a question, it is important to realize that the Gospel accounts are not eyewitness reports or unbiased historical or scientific accounts. They are popular narratives which elicit belief, at the service of the proclamation of the Gospel. Here Küng draws on the work of form criticism, a type of biblical criticism, to make distinctions between different miracle accounts—those which draw heavily on Old Testament models, those which contain elements common to Jewish and Hellenistic (Greek) miracle stories of the day, and those which contain elements to either heighten or restrain the miraculous content.

The conclusion of these form critical analyses is that within the Jesus tradition, "the coverage of miracles as a whole cannot be dismissed as unhistorical" (p.229). In fact, biblical exegetes generally accept the following as facts: that Jesus performed cures of various types of sicknesses, among them certain types of psychogenetic skin diseases which would have been described as leprosy; that certain types of psychiatric conditions which would have been described as "possession by evil spirits" were cured by Jesus; that nature miracles, such as the calming of the storm, may at least have been occasioned by historical facts.

This analysis of what happened arises out of a recognition of typical patterns of transmission of such accounts within an oral and literary tradition. This recognizes the effects of further development of the original tradition, leading to embellishments and legendary accretions. Further themes and material from outside the tradition are transferred onto Jesus, as happens with all founders of great religions. Finally, in our specifically Christian setting, the miracle stories are shot through with anticipated portrayals of the risen Jesus. It is these influences which led to our final Gospel accounts.

It becomes clear from this that Jesus' miracles cannot be seen as unequivocal proof of his messiahship or his divinity. Firstly, they are not unique in the history of religions. Secondly, even in their own time, they were seen as ambiguous signs, events which raised a question, but which did not completely answer it. It is only in the light of Jesus' preaching of the kingdom of God that the miracles take on their true significance. Through his miracles, Jesus "appears not only as a preacher, but also in word and deed as guarantor of the coming kingdom of God" (p.238).

The type of analysis that Küng gives us of the miracles of Jesus is fairly typical of the conclusions that have been drawn by modern biblical and historical criticism. They involve a detailed literary analysis of the Gospel texts, seeking to uncover the process of development from historical event to oral tradition to literary form. All the scholar has, of course, is the final literary form. However, through comparisons between Gospels and with comparable literature from other religious movements, patterns of development arise, which allow one to move back from the text to the oral tradition and finally to the historical event itself. The key danger, which Küng recognizes, is a rationalistic exclusion of certain events as impossible simply because they fall outside our own contemporary expectations.

It is in the application of these methods to the scriptural texts on the resurrection that Küng and others (e.g. Edward Schillebeeckx in his recent Christological works) have come into conflict with Church authorities. More than anything, it is this conflict which highlights the tension between modern critico-historical methodology and traditional theological formulations. It is a conflict which is yet to be fully resolved.

Comments on theological method

At this stage we should make some comments on Küng's theological method. We are helped here by the fact that Küng concludes his discussion of the reality of God with some notes on theological method (see pp.87–88). Firstly, while he describes his style as "dialectic," his starting point is not God's revelation from above, as in the dialectic theology of Karl Barth, but human experience, "from below." Küng's dialectic is an upward thrusting dialectic of critical questioning, particularly of any claims to authority.

Secondly, theology should not pretend to give a total explanation of reality. All the sciences have their own sphere of competence and these should be recognized and respected. Theology should not again find itself, as it did with Galileo, defending, not true faith, but an outmoded worldview.

Thirdly, theological method can learn from the methods of the natural sciences:

> ... arguments, information, facts, are not to be shut out; existing intellectual and social situations are not to be unconditionally authorized; there must be no partisan justification of certain

dogmas, ideological structures, even forms of social domination (p.87).

Thus Küng rejects any *a priori* intervention by the teaching office of the Church within theology. Some might say that in this comparison between the methodology of empirical science and theology Küng adopts the ideals of the scientific methodology in a too uncritical manner. The success of scientific method may have more to do with its subject matter than with its own inherent goodness and may in fact provide a poor model for theological method.

This methodological statement of Küng's is consistent with his heavy reliance on critico-historical methodology in his attempt to recover the "historical Jesus." Indeed, Küng expresses confidence that consensus can be achieved through the use of this method. In terms of the functional specialties discussed in Chapter 4, we can see that Küng's approach relies heavily on the specialties of research, interpretation and history. However, Küng's confidence that some form of consensus is possible would indicate that Küng has not paid sufficient attention to the horizon of the interpreter, the prior commitments, concerns and judgments which any interpreter brings to his or her work. It is the diversity of horizons which will by necessity give rise to a diversity of interpretations and hence the need for dialectics.

Indeed, recent events in theology have shown how shaky Küng's consensus is. Liberation Theology and Feminist Theology have raised serious doubts about the consensus achieved by predominantly middle-class European male scripture scholars that Küng draws upon.

Moreover, as his own description of his dialectic method indicates, Küng has no place in his theology for the downward thrust of God's revealing power. It is little wonder that Küng has had such problems with ecclesiastical authorities. Küng's one-sided attachment to an "ascending" theology is matched only by their attachment to a "descending" theology. Anyone who stands on one leg for too long is bound to fall over!

Küng's book, *On Being a Christian*, was a major contribution to the popularization of theology. It continues to be a thought-provoking work, even within the limitations of its methodology. There are few works which deal with the whole gamut of Christian belief and practice in such a readable yet reasonably scholarly way. However, while it contributes to the general theological debate, it should not be seen, nor would Küng want it to be seen, as offering the last word.

DISCUSSION QUESTIONS

- What do you make of Küng's claim that "we are able today to know better than perhaps any former generations of Christians—except the first—the true, original Jesus of history" (p.161)?

- If he is correct, how do you account for nineteen hundred years of Christianity between the first generation of Christians and the present?

Bibliography

As was mentioned above, Küng has written many books which are a valuable contribution to theological discussion. Of special interest are perhaps the following:
The Church, New York/London: Sheed and Ward/Search Press, 1968—a study of the New Testament data on the Church.
Does God Exist?, New York/London: Doubleday/Collins, 1978—a study of the various philosophical arguments for the existence of God, together with Küng's own position on the question. This work is a good resource since it covers many of the different philosophers who have shaped modern thought.
Eternal Life?, New York/London: Doubleday/Collins, 1984—a readable account of the problem of life after death from a variety of perspectives. This arose out of public lectures so is a non-specialist work, highly readable.
Global Responsibility: In Search of a New World Ethic, London: SCM, 1991—in light of the global problems facing humanity, particularly those of the environment, Küng draws upon the

resources of Christianity and other world religions to develop an ethic commensurate with the problem. Küng argues that there can be no world peace without religious peace and no religious peace without religious dialogue. This program has been carried out by Küng through major studies on Islam, Judaism, and now Christianity.

Mozart: Traces of Transcendence, Grand Rapids, Michigan/ London: Eerdmans/SCM Press, 1992—following an earlier study of Mozart by Karl Barth, Küng here considers the religious significance of Mozart, his life and music. He finds in Mozart's music traces of transcendence which open us up to religious experience.

Christianity: The Religious Situation of Our Time, London: SCM, 1994—following on similar studies of Judaism and Islam, here Küng explores the historical development of Christianity through various epochs and their major paradigms. Nothing if not encyclopedic, Küng sees this work as a major extension of his earlier work, *On Being a Christian*.

On the question of the historical Jesus there are also a number of good works that the reader may consult. For a diversity of styles and approaches the following may be of value:

W. Kasper, *Jesus the Christ*, New York: Paulist Press, 1976.

L. Boff, *Jesus Christ, Liberator*, Maryknoll, N.Y.: Orbis Books, 1978; London: SPCK, 1985.

J. Dunn, *Jesus and the Spirit*, London: SCM Press, 1975.

B. Meyer, *The Aims of Jesus*, London: SCM Press, 1979.

CHAPTER 6

Sebastian Moore, *Psychological Theology*

The works of Sebastian Moore live in a twilight zone between academic theology and spirituality. They are generally short books, little more than one hundred pages, with no footnotes to speak of and certainly no index of terms at the back. Though they are clearly meant for a popular audience, the writing is often dense and difficult to decipher. Still they reward those who are willing to put in the effort to read them, as they are full of rich insights into human psychology and spirituality. It is this integration of psychology and theology which makes Moore's books a significant contribution to contemporary theology.

Though Sebastian Moore had written an earlier work, *God Is a New Language*, in 1968, it was only in the later 70s and 80s that we saw the production of a series of works on the theme of an existential Christology—*The Crucified (Jesus) Is No Stranger, The Fire and the Rose Are One, The Inner Loneliness* and *Let This Mind Be in You*. Unlike Hans Küng, Moore has not written a "magnum opus," more a series of reports of "work in progress." Often his works will contain retractions and additions to earlier works. His aim in all these works is to attempt to understand the crucifixion of Jesus as the basic saving event—how does Jesus' death and resurrection save us?

Material under consideration—*The Fire and the Rose Are One*, New York/London: The Seabury Press/Darton, Longman and Todd, 1980

Of these four books, the one which I consider the clearest and the most insightful is *The Fire and the Rose Are One*. In this book, Moore sets out two questions which "control" his investigation: "How is Jesus in his climactic moment recognized by us?" and "Where should the interaction between the story of Jesus and reflectively understood human experience be studied?" In other words, Moore is asking how we recognize the death and resurrection of Jesus as our central saving event and where it is that this saving story and human experience continue to interact. In attempting to answer such questions, Moore develops a theological psychology, or a psychological theology, of the human person as a God-directed, yet at the same time God-alienated, being.

In *The Fire and the Rose*, Moore takes as his major dialogue partner the book, *The Denial of Death*, by Ernest Becker. Becker's book is a major cultural investigation of the ways in which we deny human finitude, deny death. For Becker, working in a Freudian framework, death renders the human project meaningless. The suppression of the cultural memory of death is necessary for the continuance of culture and as an alternative to despair. Thus, the human situation is essentially tragic and the heroic individual is the one who can face the tragedy and still continue to function. It is a fine example of a hermeneutics of suspicion applied to human culture.

Becker's analysis is based on two observations about the human situation—firstly, our human finitude, our utter dependence on what is not I (for example our environment, both human and physical); secondly, our hunger for meaning, our striving for significance, which Becker sees as narcissistic. For Becker, these two are opposed since our narcissism is ever threatened by our finitude, especially by death, and this is our tragedy.

Moore's starting point is this hunger for meaning or significance. Moore sees this as a fundamental and universal human need. For Moore, Becker's genius is to clarify "this essential need of the human being to feel significant, worth-full, worthy, someone" (p.7). This sense of self-worth is "the survival-instinct become human."

However, Moore pushes his analysis further than Becker. For Moore this sense of self-worth, of significance, can only come from another, i.e. I need to feel my significance for another person. Moreover, not just any person, but a significant other person, the person to whom I am drawn. Thus, Moore claims, I desire to be desired by the one I desire. I need to be myself for another:

> In sum: the universal human need in its fully adult form is the need "to be myself for another," with the word "for" referring both to my attraction to the other and to the other's attraction to me. . . . I cannot think of anything less likely to be disputed than the proposition that everyone wants to be attractive to someone they find attractive. This goes right across the board from Hitler to Jesus (p.11).

For Moore, the context of self-esteem is always intersubjective and other-fulfilling. Thus, there is no opposition between self-fulfillment and other-fulfillment. Our self-concern finds its meaning in other-concern.

So far, all we have is some interesting psychological observations. They become theological when we ask about the possibility of finding an ultimate answer to the question of our self-esteem. For Becker, there is no possible source outside the human which can provide such an answer, so that ultimately the answer is "no." Since we are dependent on what is not us, on factors beyond our control, we cannot create a transcendent meaning, one which survives the threat of death.

Moore, on the other hand, sees not denial but the opportunity of fulfillment: " . . . might it not be that my self-absorption is ultimately to find its meaning and release in knowing that I am significant for the unknown reality that is my origin?" (p.13). Moore concludes that, in fact, the human search for meaning and significance is a pre-religious love affair with God: " . . . the hunger for God's approval is built right into the human heart and cannot be got rid of" (p.36). Here we can hear an echo of the Augustinian saying, "Our hearts are restless, O

Lord, until they rest in you" and that of Blaise Pascal, "You would not seek me if you had not already found me."

It is this insight into the restlessness of the human heart which Moore finds echoed in the verses of T. S. Eliot's poem "Little Gidding," quoted in the front of *The Fire and the Rose*:

> We shall not cease from exploration
> And the end of all our exploring
> Will be to arrive where we started
> And know the place for the first time.

The place where we started is our own hunger for God. However, our hunger for God does not clearly identify the object desired—it is as though through a glass, darkly. It simply sets us on our life's journey, a journey of exploration seeking the one who can fill our hearts. At journey's end, we come to realize that all along it was God that we sought, and we come to know God and ourselves for the first time.

As Moore readily acknowledges, this picture of our relationship with God is only half the story. While it is true that we are God-seeking beings, there is also within us a radical alienation from God, what tradition calls "original sin." Moore speaks of this in various ways—as a primal guilt, our original cosmic love affair with God gone sour, a deep sense of having failed the other, a disaffection with creaturehood. While the central question of our being is that posed by our need for esteem from the other, deep within us is a radical self-disesteem which threatens our quest for affirmation from the other. It is interesting to note here that the Hebrew word Satan means "the Accuser," such accusations being those which constantly undermine our feelings of self-worth. These feelings of self-disesteem cast a shadow on our relationships with God and our fellows. To quote Moore:

> The experience of original sin is produced by the withdrawing of the self from its primordial leanings towards ultimate mystery into an absolutely isolated selfhood. So far I have equated the guilt of original sin with original sin itself, making of that guilt a radical condition which one could not go behind to a sin causing the guilt. I would now say that just as inter-human guilt

is at least logically preceded by the "sin" of withdrawing into isolated self-awareness, so the deeper guilt in respect of our very being is at least logically preceded by the sin of withdrawing into isolated self-awareness in respect of the mystery on which we in fact draw for all our sense of meaning and value (p.67).

In this work, Moore does not enter into speculation about the origin of this "withdrawing into isolated self-awareness" with regard to an original "sin" of our human progenitors, Adam and Eve. It is an area he has taken up in various research papers and to some extent in *Let This Mind Be in You*. At one stage, for those with a creationist frame of mind, Moore makes the provocative statement "to not believe in evolution is not to believe in original sin"!

The question which remains to be addressed is: "How does Jesus save us from this original guilt?" Moore is not asking here for some magic formula, some waving of a magic wand which removes stains on souls. He is concerned with the real psychological processes which the death and resurrection of Jesus initiated firstly in Jesus' disciples and further on into the Church. It is this burning issue which is the common thread in all Moore's works.

Moore's starting point in answering this problem is to examine the person of Jesus. Here we find not the detailed critico-historical method of Hans Küng, but a more speculative psychological reconstruction which takes as its starting point the sinlessness of Jesus. Of all human beings, apart from Mary (Moore considers the situation of Mary and the Immaculate Conception on pp.112–114), Jesus is the one "without sin," a guiltless human being. Moore asks "what sort of behavior can we expect from one whose existence is not dogged by the primal guilt we all experience?" Such a person would experience a total, unimpeded intimacy with God; such a person would be fully open to others as persons, and not objects to be manipulated as sources of forced affirmation; such a person would have the sense that God was inaugurating something new, a new age for humankind. Moore finds these characteristics amply verified in the Gospel accounts of Jesus.

Moreover, as the Gospel accounts make clear, Jesus communicated his experience of intimacy with the Father to his disciples, initiating them into a new relationship with God—Jesus makes God come alive to the disciples. For the disciples, this creates an ambiguous situation. Firstly, there is the possibility of having their deepest human needs for affirmation fulfilled through intimate contact with God-in-Jesus. Secondly, however, the closeness of the light brings the shadow of our original human guilt into sharper focus. Jesus' freedom from guilt threatens us, calls us out of our complacency, opens up vistas of human transcendence which demand discipline and self-sacrifice. He calls us beyond our primal sense of guilt with the promise of the Spirit, affirming us with the love of God flooding our heart.

This threat is most clearly seen in the reaction of the Jewish authorities who have Jesus done away with. For the disciples, the death of Jesus brings to crisis point their ambiguous situation. The God they had experienced as alive in the message and life of Jesus, they now experience as powerless in the face of evil. For the disciples, the death of Jesus is nothing less than the death of God—only a God who has been experienced as alive can be experienced as dead!

On the other hand, the death of Jesus also erases the threat that Jesus had posed. He has been sacrificed to our own sense of inadequacy, got rid of so that we can return to the security of mediocrity. For the disciples, the death of Jesus precipitates a crisis which Moore compares with the dark night of the soul. Both desire and threat have been killed. The Good Friday/Easter Saturday experience is one of desolation:

> Not only is sin or guilt present in the pure state, but sin or guilt is wholly translated into desolation, wholly realized as desolation. The sense of failing another has got swallowed up in a sense of total isolation, that aching emptiness of the person that is always the source of guilt (p.144).

The balloon has popped and there is nothing left to do but go back fishing!

It is in this experience of desolation that the resurrection of Jesus bursts through with the gift of awakened desire. As Moore says, Jesus does what only God can do—in the resurrection appearances, he lifts the burden of primal guilt with forgiving love and rekindles a new purified desire for God in the hearts of the disciples. It is this "doing what only God can do" which Moore sees as the grounding experience for the Church's later credal formulation at Nicea—that Jesus is *homoousion*, i.e. of one substance, with the Father.

Further, Moore argues that unless the proclamation of the divinity of Jesus is grounded in such an experience, we can never shake off the suspicion of its being merely a creation of the early Church. Thus, he argues against those who see the proclamation of Jesus' divinity as something which "evolved" in the early Church without any grounding experience. Such an "evolutionary" hypothesis is not uncommon in biblical exegesis.

In a sense, Moore is here providing a psychological interpretation of the classical soteriological model of Anselm (soteriology being the theology of salvation). Anselm asked why must there be a God-man—*cur Deus homo*? His answer was as follows: human sin gives offence to God; the measure of the offence is the measure of the one offended, who is God, and hence is infinite; humankind must make amends to God, but of itself is unable to do so; Jesus, as both human and divine, can make amends to God, on the part of humankind, and give his act of atonement infinite value, since he is divine. Later interpretations of Anselm spoke of Jesus' sacrifice appeasing the anger of God.

For Moore, however, the "anger of God" is a projection onto God of our own self-disesteem, our own primal "anger" at our creaturehood. In that anger, God is no longer experienced as mystery, but as a threat who must be removed. Jesus is then a "substitutory" sacrifice, one whom in his humanity we can destroy but who in his divinity takes the place of the unseen Father:

> The causal connection of sin with the death of God is sin's requirement of the death of God for its absolving, such is sin's depth ... As people involved in the primal guilt, we call, in a way we hardly understand, for the death of God (p.146).

The death of God-in-Jesus appeases our primal anger, but also brings about our ultimate desolation. With the death of

God there is no longer the possibility of the affirmation of our being, which only God can give. It is in this desolation, this silence, that there arises the "possibility of knowing the touch of God without guilt, of knowing the voice of God without fear" (p.145). For the disciples, the touch of the risen Jesus was such a touch of God, his voice the voice of God.

Given our comments in Chapter 1 about the relationship between theology and culture, it is interesting to note that Moore includes in his analysis some comments on present Western culture. While Becker speaks of it as death–denying, Moore characterizes it more as love–denying. Indeed, he notes that "none of our great philosophies is centered on love" (p.43). In general, there is a "non-permission by the culture for the articulation, as central to human life, of what everyone is after." Our love-centeredness is thus relegated to the private sphere, whereas the public sphere denies its importance. Where the centrality of the human spirit is not a public matter, culture falls over into materialism. To such a culture, Moore claims, the Gospel is irrelevant, though not of course to its hapless prisoner, the human person caught up in consumerism as an escape from inner emptiness. Thus, Moore says, we must avoid "the awful blunder of adjusting the Gospel to make it relevant to the culture" (p.44), for to such a culture Christianity is simply irrelevant. Instead, Christianity has the role of a chaplain to an "inordinately selfish and world-devouring culture."

Comments on theological method

At this stage, I would like to make some comments on Moore's theological method. Here we are helped by some initial comments made by him on the nature of theology. Moore gives a thumbnail sketch of the history of theology by dividing it into four eras. The first is that of the Fathers of the Church. This involves retelling the story of salvation using "all the art of the story-teller, imagination, myth" (p.3). The next stage, Scholasticism, involves the movement out of myth and into reason. What do we mean by God, sin, salvation? This involves a systematic synthesis of the basic Christian themes. The next stage, initiated by Luther, shifts attention to the human experience—

what is it like to be lost or saved? This gives rise to a theological pluralism, since the variety of human experience gives many answers to each question—Feminist, Black, Liberation theologies. The fourth and final stage seeks the deeper unity within this diversity of human experience.

This is what Moore is attempting. He is attempting to find the deeper unity which grounds the diversity of human experience. In part he finds this unity in the human psyche, from which arise all our myths and symbols. Basically, Moore takes myth seriously. This does not mean taking it literally, as do the fundamentalists. More importantly, it means not rejecting myth as simply a primitive form of expression now to be taken over by a more scientific world view, as claims the rationalist. To take myth seriously is to take it seriously as myth, analyzing it according to the canons of mythology, using the insights of depth psychology (e.g. Freud and Jung). In doing so, Moore is able to interpret the myths of the first stage, to ground the categories of the second stage, and to find the unity within the third stage. This is a significant theological achievement. One possible shortcoming, however, is that the analysis of the myths given by Moore remains predominantly from the perspective of the male psyche.

In terms of the functional specialties mentioned in Chapter 4, Moore's work falls into the area of foundations. His task is a foundational one, seeking to give expression to the basic experiences of conversion, particularly the experience of religious conversion as mediated by the death and resurrection of Jesus. What distinguishes Moore's writing from that of other foundational writers (such as Rahner) is his sensitivity to the issues of psychic conversion. The categories he uses to express this experience of religious conversion are not the metaphysics of Aristotle or Aquinas, but the psychological categories of self-esteem and disesteem, of guilt and anger, of falling in love, and the myths and symbols which give expression to these.

DISCUSSION QUESTIONS

- Discuss the various meanings which the word "myth" may have. Give an account of the relationship between myth and religion.

- Give your own account of how Jesus saves us. Can your recognize mythic elements in your own account?

Bibliography

As was mentioned in the opening material for this chapter, Moore has written a number of books dealing with an "existential Christology" and its various ramifications.
The Crucified [Jesus] Is No Stranger, New York/London: Seabury Press/Darton, Longman and Todd, 1977—a difficult work with some brilliant material on the experience of sin and human failure. However, Moore himself moves away from the soteriological analysis he presents in this work, as we see in *The Fire and the Rose Are One*. This book has recently been reprinted by Seabury Press.
The Inner Loneliness, New York/London: Crossroad/Darton, Longman and Todd, 1982—Moore's analysis of human alienation from God leads him to explore the specifically sexual ramifications of that alienation. Further, he explores the significance of the doctrine of the Trinity to our inner loneliness.
Let This Mind Be in You, New York/London: Seabury Press/Darton, Longman and Todd, 1985—Moore further explores the significance of original sin, with special reference to the Oedipus crisis.
   For another analysis of Moore's work see:
D. Edwards, *What Are They Saying about Salvation?*, New York: Paulist Press, 1986.
   For a similar theological style, dealing with similar issues, see:
R. Haughton, *The Passionate God*, London: Darton, Longman and Todd, 1981.

CHAPTER 7

Edward Schillebeeckx, *Reinterpreting the Past*

Edward Schillebeeckx is one of the major theologians of the twentieth century. He has made significant, major and epochal contributions to theology for well over thirty years. His most significant works include *Christ the Sacrament of Encounter with God; Marriage, Secular Reality and Saving Mystery; The Eucharist; Ministry; Jesus, An Experiment in Christology; Christ, The Christian Experience in the Modern World*. He is the leading theologian of the Dutch Church and made significant contributions to Vatican II. His works on Christology and ministry have led to tensions with the Sacred Congregation for Doctrine and Faith which remain unresolved. Unlike Küng, Schillebeeckx has been willing to enter into extensive dialogue with Vatican officials, some of which has been published.

The work we are considering here, *The Eucharist*, also caused controversy when it appeared. In a sense, it was a public statement of a debate which had been going on both covertly and overtly for some years prior to its publication. Schillebeeckx gives a history of the debate in Chapter 2 of this work (see pp.107–121). The debate captures many of the elements which are central to contemporary theology—recognition of the role of history and culture, hermeneusis of past beliefs into the present, the shift from metaphysics to philosophical anthropology. In one sense, the success or failure of this particular project is not as significant as the actual attempt to integrate the various shifts involved.

It is important to note that the book, *The Eucharist*, belongs to an earlier stage in Schillebeeckx's theological development. I have chosen it because of the importance of the topic it deals with, and because of the manner in which it illustrates questions dealing with theological method. Since that time, Schillebeeckx has undergone dramatic changes in his approach, becoming even more immersed in hermeneutic and political questions. I shall make some further comments on this shift at the end of this chapter.

Material under consideration—*The Eucharist*, London: Sheed and Ward, 1968

The book consists of two chapters. The first deals with a hermeneusis of the doctrine of transubstantiation and real presence, as taught at the Council of Trent. This is the material we shall primarily focus on. The second seeks to reinterpret the real presence within a contemporary framework. It argues for the concept of "transignification" as an alternative to transubstantiation.

Schillebeeckx begins his discussion with a distinction between what is really affirmed in any particular doctrine and its "wording" or manner of presentation, which "in those past times ... was vital to the question of whether the statement concerning the faith was or was not true" (p.26). He is not suggesting that the people from the past who formulated doctrines were necessarily aware of such a distinction. Indeed, for them, what was being affirmed was only accessible through their own formulation. The reality being affirmed is mediated by meaning, i.e. reality is accessible only through human acts of understanding. A problem arises only for later generations which are not familiar with the thought forms of the past and hence must make such a distinction if they are to be able to express the real affirmation in their own day. Otherwise we are canonizing not the dogmas of the past but their thought forms!

Schillebeeckx then proceeds with a detailed analysis and exegesis of the text of the Council of Trent. The purpose of this process is to attempt to recover the "intention of the authors" i.e. what was the intention of the Council in its formulation of the canons on the real presence of Christ in the Eucharist? To gauge this intention, Schillebeeckx considers the various debates and draft formulations which led up to the final canons. This sort of detailed analysis is a good example of the exegetical task which seeks to uncover the intention of the text through a consideration of its immediate history, setting and context as well as the actual words themselves. It is only within this immediate history, setting and context that the words can mediate the meaning intended by their authors.

As a point of historical interest, it is significant to note that this type of analysis of the documents of Trent has been possible only in this century. After the Council of Trent, the documentation of the debates was withheld from view, placed in Vatican archives with only very restricted access. The aim, it seems, was to present a united front after the divisive times of the Reformation, by burying the very real differences among Catholics revealed in the debates at the Council. It has only been since the pontificate of Leo XIII (1878-1903) that access to the debates of Trent has been possible and that the type of analysis that Schillebeeckx offers could be done.

After passing through several "editions," the final form of the Tridentine canons which Schillebeeckx considers is as follows:

1. If anyone should deny that the most holy sacrament of the Eucharist truly, really and substantially contains the body and blood together with the soul and divinity of our Lord Jesus Christ and thus the whole Christ, but should say that they . . . are only [present] as in a sign or figure or [only] by efficacy, let him be anathema.

2. Should anyone maintain that in the most holy sacrament of the Eucharist the substance of bread and wine remains [in existence] together with the body and blood of our Lord Jesus Christ and should deny this wonderful and unique changing of the whole substance of bread into the body and of the whole substance of wine into the blood while the species of bread and wine nonetheless remains, which change the Catholic Church very suitably calls transubstantiation, let him be anathema (pp.37–38).

Schillebeeckx discerns three different levels in these Tridentine affirmations:

1. An "affirmation of a specific and distinctive eucharistic presence" so that Christ is "really, truly and substantially present" (p.44) in the sacrament.

2. That this presence could be expressed in no other way than as a change of the substance of bread and wine into the substance of the body and blood of Christ.

3. That this change was suitably called transubstantiation.

However, it is not as if the Church fathers at Trent were necessarily aware of these distinct levels. For them the eucharistic "real presence" and transubstantiation were simply identical. It is ahistorical to suggest that the Council Fathers could have put aside their Aristotelian scholasticism and produced a pure statement of faith. It is only for a later generation, for which Aristotelian metaphysics (as opposed to Aristotelian language!) is no longer current, that such a disassociation must occur.

Schillebeeckx finds a similar three-level distinction in the work of Thomas Aquinas on the eucharistic presence.

1. A faith statement on the uniqueness of the eucharistic presence.

2. An ontological statement on the change of being from bread and wine to the body and blood of Christ.

3. An analysis of the change in terms of Aristotle's metaphysics of substance and accidents.

While Schillebeeckx feels safe in asserting that the third level in both Trent and Aquinas is secondary and relative, the question he sees as basic is whether the second level, that of an ontological change is essential or is simply part of the "wording" of the canon—"In my opinion, this question brings us to the very heart of the modern problem" (p.65).

This leads Schillebeeckx to the inevitable question—what is reality? (p.76) How are we to understand reality, so as to be able to make sense of the notion of an ontological change, a change of being or reality? This is not a peripheral question, but central to any understanding of the Eucharist. It should, however, be noted that it is basically a philosophical question, though Schillebeeckx's analysis is highly theological.

Indeed, for Schillebeeckx, this philosophical question cannot be separated from questions of faith—"our view of reality cannot possibly be separated completely from our conviction of faith" (p.78). In exploring this issue he refers to the work of a Calvinist theologian, F. J. Leenhardt. For Leenhardt, things are what they are because God says so! This word of God, however, remains purely extrinsic; it does not change the thing itself. Thus, we discover the reality of the thing not by attending to it, or by experiencing it, but by attending to God, to God's intention:

> . . . the true reality of something is . . . thus situated in what God gives to man through these things. The truth or reality of things is therefore not to be found in these things themselves, in what we, as men, see and experience of these things: "the substance of a reality is in the divine intention which is realised in it" (p.77).

Philosophically, this position is similar to that of Kant. Our human experience of things, through our senses, our understanding, does not lead us to the "truth or reality of things." This remains hidden, a noumenal reality. However, unlike Kant, for Leenhardt this reality is accessible through faith, through attending to God's intention—"only faith, then, is able to grasp this substantial reality" (p.77).

For Schillebeeckx, however, the Catholic view is that reality is not an extrinsic relation to an object, i.e. a thing is so because God decrees it so, but an intrinsic realization of such a relation, i.e. the thing is in its own being a realization of such a relation:

> This view of reality is clearly very different from the Catholic view. It is, of course, true that we would not disagree with Leenhardt's primary affirmation, that God himself is the ultimate ground on which all reality is founded, that reality is what it is by divine constitution. But the Catholic view of reality cannot admit the "extrinsicism" of the creative word of God. He claims in addition that through this creative word things are what they are in an absolute and inward manner (p.78).

Thus, he concludes that, indeed, an ontological change in the bread and wine is central to the Tridentine affirmation of faith.

Before we move from this point, we might well ask what is behind this question of extrinsic and intrinsic relations to objects. The prior issue here is not Protestant and Catholic differences on the Eucharist, but Catholic and Protestant differences on justification, the key issue of the Reformation. Luther held, or at least Catholics believed Luther to hold, that the process of justification of the sinner, brought about by faith, produced no inner change in the sinner. The sinner remained a sinner even though God, in an extrinsic manner, treated the sinner as if he or she were justified, because of the merits of Christ. Catholics, on the other hand, believe that the sinner undergoes a real and inner (intrinsic) change in the process of justification.

At the same time, Schillebeeckx registers a protest against viewing this eucharistic change in too "objective" a manner, outside the sacramental context in which it occurs. It is a faith reality, a change not accessible to some type of scientific analysis, but one grasped through the transforming light of the Holy Spirit.

The second part of the book deals with Schillebeeckx's attempt to formulate this ontological change in the categories of modern philosophy, which are not so concerned with substance as with meaning—hence the term transignification, or change in meaning (also transvaluation—change in value).

In this section, Schillebeeckx carries out a twofold critique of the concept of substance. The first prong of the critique, a hermeneutics of suspicion, notes how the term "substance" has been debased in modern philosophy. It has come to take on a very physical meaning, as when we speak of a physical or chemical substance, so that when people spoke of transubstantiation in the Eucharist they thought that this implied a physical or chemical change, one discernible through scientific means. However, the eucharistic change is not "physical" in this sense but "metaphysical." If the term "substance" indeed takes on this "physical" meaning, then transubstantiation is not a proper way of speaking about the eucharistic presence.

On the other hand, Schillebeeckx also engages in a hermeneutics of recovery, an attempt to recover a more authentic meaning of the word "substance." He notes the work of B.

Welte, who investigates other shades of meaning of the term "substance," such as when we speak of the substantial reality of a thing under investigation. Here Schillebeeckx gives the example of a coloured cloth which is adopted as a nation's flag. In its adoption as a flag, the substantial reality of the thing has changed. It no longer is just a piece of coloured cloth, but is in fact a national flag, something that can attract deep loyalties and evoke profound feelings. In such a case the "substance" of the thing has changed, there has been a "transubstantiation."

However, rather than use the term "substance" and what he considers a problematic Aristotelian metaphysics of substance and accident (species, in the Tridentine formulation), Schillebeeckx seeks to understand the Eucharist in terms of an analysis of the notion of sign. Using the distinction between noumenon and phenomenon, between the reality itself and the form in which it appears, he presents an analysis which sees the phenomena as a sign, as a way of giving meaning to us, of the noumenal reality of the thing itself. Thus, normally the appearances of bread and wine, their phenomena, are a sign of the reality of bread and wine. However, in the Eucharist, these same phenomena become a sign for a new reality, the reality of the body and blood of Christ:

> The phenomenal form of the eucharistic bread and wine is nothing other than the sign which makes real Christ's gift of himself with the Church's responding gift of herself involved in making real to us, a sign inviting every believer to participate personally in this event (p.139).

Thus, in the Eucharist, the change in sign or meaning of the phenomena of bread and wine amounts to a transignification. It is important to note that Schillebeeckx is not denying transubstantiation. In fact, he sees transubstantiation and transignification as very closely related. His concern is with effecting a shift from a metaphysical analysis to an anthropological one, where the categories of sign and meaning "take over" the metaphysical categories of accidents and substance.

There are, of course, many other issues that could be raised concerning Schillebeeckx's analysis of the Eucharist, of transubstantiation and transignification. As with all the theologians considered in this book, I am more concerned with a consideration of methods and the shifts in perspective that the various works illustrate—from classicism to historical consciousness, from metaphysics to anthropology, from dogmatism to hermeneutics.

Comments on theological method

As with Küng, Schillebeeckx is employing a critico-historical methodology, though, as I set out below, he carries it much further than Küng. The main difference from Küng is that Schillebeeckx is not dealing with scriptural texts but with dogmatic decrees. The problem of "hermeneutics of dogma" remains a problematic one for Catholic theology, one which has been, and will continue to be, a source of controversy.

As I note above, Schillebeeckx pushes the critico-historical methodology much further than Küng. In order to illustrate this, it is of interest to note how well Schillebeeckx's method illustrates the various functional specialties referred to in Chapter 4 of this work. The basic research work was done by those scholars who edited the debates of the Council of Trent and made them accessible to the theological world. Schillebeeckx then seeks to interpret the canons of the Council in the light of this basic research, so as to be able to make an historical judgment about the intention of the Council. Inasmuch as these canons refer to the Eucharist, Schillebeeckx turns his attention to this reality and notes a variety of interpretations about it (dialectics), especially differences between Catholics and Protestants. These differences he grounds in differing understandings of reality, in Lonergan's terms, in the presence or absence of intellectual conversion.

Schillebeeckx then concludes that his faith stance commits him to a particular philosophical position, one which sees meaning as an intrinsic component of reality so that reality is accessible through human acts of meaning. This is a foundational position from which his theology will flow. He thus concludes that it was part of the intention of the doctrine of Trent to affirm an ontological change of the bread and wine as part of the eucharistic mystery. Schillebeeckx then proceeds to give a systematic understanding of this mystery in terms of his philosophical anthropology, in which meaning is a significant category, rather than the traditional metaphysical approach which used the category of substance. He does this because he judges that the category of meaning will communicate the reality of the eucharistic mystery more readily to contemporary culture than the category of substance.

Schillebeeckx's foundational principle receives further elucidation in the second part of his book, where he presents his own systematic on the eucharistic change. There he adopts the language of noumenon and phenomenon, of the reality itself and the form or appearance of the reality. Though the language is that of Kant, the fact that Schillebeeckx sees reality as accessible through human understanding would indicate that philosophically his position is more that of a Platonic rather than a Kantian idealist.

However, in my opinion, Schillebeeckx, in his later works, moves away from the foundational principle which he develops in his work on Eucharist. While maintaining that reality is intrinsic to the object, he seems to me to adopt a more Kantian position that this reality is no longer accessible to human knowing, that human knowing is merely a projection onto the object whose inner reality remains hidden from us. The reader might like to read the relevant material in the book *Christ, The Christian Experience in the Modern World* (see especially pp.31–54) and make his or her own decision.

DISCUSSION QUESTIONS

- Do you think that the Church should maintain the use of traditional terms such as "transubstantiation" in its preaching despite changes in culture? Why?

- Terms such as "substance" and "significance" have diverse connotations. Can you explain how these implications could give rise to diverse theological understandings of the eucharistic presence?

Bibliography

As was noted in the beginning of this chapter, Schillebeeckx has written many works dealing with the Church, sacraments and Christology. Below are just a few notes on some of these works.

Jesus, An Experiment in Christology, New York/London: Crossroad/Collins, 1979—the first in a proposed three-volume work on Jesus, this volume applies a critico-historical methodology and various theological criteria to analyze the Synoptic Gospel accounts of the ministry, death and resurrection of Jesus. It is a long and exhaustive work, which has suffered in translation. However, it is an excellent resource on the then current state of research on the historical Jesus. His handling of the resurrection led Schillebeeckx into some difficulties with the Sacred Congregation for the Doctrine of the Faith.

Christ, The Christian Experience in the Modern World, New York/London: Crossroad/SCM Press, 1980—the second volume of the above, in which Schillebeeckx examines the remaining New Testament books as witnesses of the ongoing life of grace initiated by Jesus in the Church. This is then supplemented by more contemporary reflection on the life of grace, as experienced in our present situation. Again, it is a long and exhaustive work, over nine hundred pages, but an excellent resource.

Church: The Human Story of God, New York: Crossroad, 1990—this is the third volume of the Christological trilogy Schillebeeckx originally conceived in writing *Jesus*. The foreword contains some rather pointed comments on the present state of the Church. However the work as a whole attempts to link the existence and mission of the Church to the historical praxis of Jesus.

Ministry, New York/London: Crossroad/SCM Press, 1981, and *The Church with a Human Face*, New York/London: Crossroad/SCM Press, 1985—both works deal with the question of ministry in the Church. Indeed *The Church with a Human Face* is an expanded and revised edition of the work *Ministry*. Both works consider the historical expressions of priestly ministry within the Church, from the early Church to the present day. Schillebeeckx's views on priestly ministry, in particular his position concerning the celebration of Eucharist in a situation of a shortage of priests (refer to our chapter on Boff), led to problems again with the Sacred Congregation for the Doctrine of the Faith. The second work seeks to clarify his position.

The books above represent the latest stage of Schillebeeckx's theological development. As I noted in the introduction to this chapter, the work we have considered, *The Eucharist*, and his well-known *Christ the Sacrament of Encounter with God*, London: Sheed and Ward, 1963, belong to an earlier and, to some extent, less sophisticated era. In any theologian's work, it is important to recognize development, both of ideas and of methodology!

Also of interest is the autobiographical essay:
I am a Happy Theologian, London: SCM Press, 1994.

For a sympathetic treatment of Schillebeeckx, his life and work, read:
J. Bowden, *Edward Schillebeeckx, Portrait of a Theologian*, London: SCM Press, 1983.
P. Kennedy, *Schillebeeckx*, London: Geoffrey Chapman, 1993.

CHAPTER 8

Wolfhart Pannenberg, *Systematic Theology*

Wolfhart Pannenberg is a leading German Protestant theologian of the second half of the twentieth century. Belonging to the Lutheran tradition, he was Professor of Systematic Theology at the University of Munich from 1968 to 1994. He has written widely in theology, dealing with the full range of theological issues. His early works dealt with the theology of revelation, where he promoted the idea of history as revelatory. He authored a major Christological book, *Jesus—God and Man* and, as a culmination of his long career, he has produced his major work, *Systematic Theology*, in three densely argued volumes.

His theology has developed out of an ongoing dialogue with other leading Protestant theologians such as Friedrich Schleiermacher, Karl Barth and Rudolph Bultmann, as well as with a German philosophical tradition based on Kant, Hegel and Heidegger. He also has an expert knowledge of the Scholastic past, particularly of Duns Scotus. Pannenberg has also shown a strong interest in science and the humanities. In many ways he is a modern "Renaissance man," someone with a working familiarity with a wide range of scholarly and scientific disciplines.

Unlike many Protestant theologians his theology has a strong philosophical, even metaphysical, content. Here he is responding to the same types of issues raised by the process philosophy of Alfred Whitehead, those of the relationship between God and creation. However, he strongly rejects the answers proposed by process thought, seeing them as compromising the divine transcendence. His lifelong concern has been to develop an ontology (philosophy of being) in which Jesus' eschatological vision of the Kingdom of God has a central place. In doing so he shows us that he is as much at home with abstruse metaphysical questions about the divine nature as he is with questions of Scriptural exegesis.

As with his contemporary, Jürgen Moltmann, Pannenberg can be described as an eschatological theologian, that is, one for whom the theology of the end-time is pivotal for Christian self-understanding. However, that shall not be the focus here. Instead I shall consider Pannenberg as one of the rare breed of truly systematic theologians.

Material Under Consideration—*An Introduction to Systematic Theology*, Grand Rapids, Michigan: Eerdmans, 1991

As is the case with many well-known German theologians, both Catholic and Protestant, Pannenberg's works can make for difficult reading, even for a professional theologian. We are fortunate, therefore, that in 1991 he published a series of public lectures on the topic of systematic theology. This brief work, *An Introduction to Systematic Theology*, a mere sixty-nine pages in length, provides an accessible and succinct introduction to the main themes of his theology.

For Pannenberg, the fundamental question to be faced is "why an individual person should commit herself or himself to be a member of the Christian Church" (p.3). The answer to this question itself depends on a question of truth: only if the God of Israel and Jesus is the true God can we reasonably commit ourselves to be members of the Christian Church. Everything depends, then, on the reality of this God. The story of Jesus must, at its core, be historical, not mythical, and the God of Jesus must be real and not mythical, if we are to entrust ourselves to him.

This then is the rationale, according to Pannenberg, for doing systematic theology. The question of truth is not initially theological, since to "most people, beauty speaks of truth in more powerful ways than any intellectual argument does." However, in the long term, only a systematic theology can answer the question of truth. It does so by establishing the coherence of faith in the God of Jesus:

> Coherence provides the final criterion of truth, and it can serve as such a criterion because it also belongs to the nature of truth: Whatever is true must finally be consistent with all other truth, so that truth is only one, but all-embracing, closely related to the concept of the one God (p.6).

The possibility of a coherent systematic presentation of faith, as achieved in a truly systematic theology, becomes then a criterion for the truth of Christian faith. And the most illuminating example of such a coherent presentation of faith occurs in the doctrine of God, "the most comprehensive subject of systematic theology" (p.8).

Pannenberg's starting point for talking about God is to conceive God as the power upon which all finite reality depends, the power which determines everything, but is itself not determined apart from "self-imposed forms of limitation." This conception of divinity causes him to reject the process philosophy of Whitehead. In process thought God is limited by a world which is not strictly God's creation. In contrast to this process view, the goal of a systematic theology of God is, according to Pannenberg, to give us confidence that the world "is indeed susceptible of a coherent interpretation as being created by God" (p.10).

However, systematic theology is not limited to this. God not only creates the world, God also sustains it in existence and redeems it from ultimate annihilation. Indeed this final redemptive act of God is "part and parcel of the demonstration of the reality of God" (p.12). God proves his existence to us by leading creation to its final eschatological consummation. Only in the eschaton is God's creative work complete and his existence clearly demonstrated. Theology must demonstrate the coherence of all these aspects of divinity, both internally and with what science tells us of the world.

Pannenberg notes that within Christian history many others, most notably Thomas Aquinas, have attempted such a synthesis of Christian faith. However, there are factors in our contemporary culture which give this task an added importance. In particular, modern culture no longer recognizes an authoritative tradition. The teaching of the Church and even the Scriptures themselves are reduced to a merely human authority. As a result there is an even greater need for a systematic theology to present the coherence of the truth presented authoritatively in the Scriptures. In this way systematic theology can prevent faith from becoming a purely personal retreat into subjectivism.

Still, such systematic theological knowledge remains imperfect. The question of truth remains open, something we cannot guarantee before we even start to theologize. Only God can "prove definitively his reality" and we must leave it to God to do so. The task of systematic theology is to establish the coherence of faith, not only within itself but with the "wealth of insight gained by the secular disciplines into the mysteries of nature, of human life and history" (p.18). Only in this way can the truth claims of our faith be restated in our contemporary world.

A key step in achieving this is, according to Pannenberg, to restate the doctrine of God in terms of rational argument. Inevitably this will require a revision of classical metaphysical language about God. Pannenberg notes the current trend away from metaphysics in both theology and philosophy, with the exception of process philosophy, which he rejects, but he urges theologians to participate in current philosophical dialogue with the metaphysical tradition. For, throughout the history of Christian thought, metaphysics has played a crucial role in keeping theological language honest, "as far as rational plausibility was concerned" (p.25).

As part of his own contribution to this dialogue, Pannenberg criticizes the previous efforts of Paul Tillich and Bishop John Robinson (in his work, *Honest to God*) for failing to account for the *personal* character of God, as conceived in the Christian tradition. In particular he draws attention to the trinitarian character of Christian faith:

> The Christian faith does not speak of God as one person but rather as three persons. The divine essence as such was not conceived as person. The one God is personal only with regard to

the concreteness of his trinitarian life in the interactions of Father, Son and Spirit (p.26).

In this we see something of the novelty of Pannenberg's approach. The ontology he seeks to develop is not something simply found through rational reflection. It incorporates a faith perspective, specifically, a trinitarian faith perspective. This distinguishes his approach from more classical ones where faith (theology) and reason (philosophy) were more carefully distinguished. Here we see a much greater interpenetration of the two.

In this regard Pannenberg has some interesting things to say about the trinitarian nature of God. He notes that this "concretely personal way of relating to God is made accessible only by revelation" (p.31). He concludes from this concrete reference that it would be incorrect to think of the term "Father" as an exchangeable metaphor, with the same status as words such as "mother" or "friend":

> In the Christian language about God, the word "Father" indicates that our way of talking about God and of addressing God relates to the same God whom Jesus talked about. . . . Where the word "Father" is replaced by something else, there can be no warrant anymore that we are talking about and addressing the same God as Jesus did (pp.31–32).

Similarly the word "Son" is derived from "Father" as a personal name of the second person of the Trinity, and it is only in relation to both that the Spirit can be considered personal also. He concludes that any exchange of the name "Father" by something else "inevitably results in turning to another God" (p.32). Jesus' use of the term "Father" exhibits a finality which transcends the guesswork of normal human symbolic language. Rather it reflects the divine reality itself. These are not conclusions that most feminist theologians would accept.

This discussion of the tripersonal nature of God leads Pannenberg to reflect further on the nature of personhood. Here he is very critical of the traditional idea of God as mind, where person is understood according to the definition of Boethius as "an individual substance of an intellectual nature." Since the time of Augustine, and particularly in the work of Aquinas, theologians have developed a psychological analogy for the Trinity based on the activities of the human mind and will. However, Pannenberg argues, along with Spinoza, that once the limitations of the human mind and will are removed, there is no longer any basis for an analogy. He further refers to the criticism of Fichte that such an approach makes of God a projection of the human.

Pannenberg sees these as devastating criticisms of the Western notion of God as mind, which he dismisses as anthropomorphic. Moreover, he does not accept that this western tradition adequately represents the Biblical conception of God as spirit. For in Biblical languages "spirit" does not mean "mind." Rather the connotation is of wind or breath. He prefers to see the Biblical notion of spirit as "close to the intuition of an infinite field of power" (p.35). Further he argues that the Biblical notion of the divine will is not dependent upon intellect and that passages referring to divine knowledge have a metaphorical character.

Pushing these ideas further Pannenberg, in opposition to traditional theology, seeks to give each of the persons of the Trinity their own unique role in the process of creation. Here creation is understood not as a static act of establishing the world but as a dynamic, evolving process where new forms emerge with the same sense of contingency as historical events. How then is a trinitarian God related to such a process?

Again Pannenberg rejects the traditional Western approach which would attempt to answer such a question by reference to God's mind and will. Rather, he adopts the Biblical idea of the Son cooperating in creation. In the act of distinguishing himself from the Father, the Son may be thought of as the origin of everything that is different from God:

The eternal act of the Son's self-differentiation from the Father would then contain the possibility of the separate existence of creatures. As the self-distinction of the Son from the Father is to be regarded as an act of freedom, so the contingency in the production of creatures would be in continuity with such freedom (p.42).

In this way the Logos-Son would be conceived as a generative principle of otherness.

This same approach is extended to the role of the Holy Spirit in creation. Previously Pannenberg had discussed the Biblical notion of spirit in terms of a field of force. He now traces the history of the idea in philosophy by noting its relationship to the Stoic idea of *pneuma* (Greek for spirit). The Stoics conceived of spirit as an all-pervasive material element, more subtle than air, extending throughout space. Early in Christian history such an understanding was rejected by Origen as too materialistic. However, Pannenberg in turn rejects Origen's Platonism as an intellectualist reduction of the Biblical view.

Instead Pannenberg prefers to conceive of the Holy Spirit as "the supreme field of power that pervades all creation" (p.46). This field of power is seen in the ecstatic self-transcendence of life and of spiritual experience in particular. Indeed every finite event and being is a manifestation of that field and responsive to its forces. In this way all actions of God in history and nature can be considered as "field effects." This language allows Pannenberg to relate his theological description of nature to that of the world of physics, with its notions of space, time and energy:

> If the notion of energy can also be related to this concept of spirit as field, the presence of God's Spirit in his creation can be described as a field of creative presence, a comprehensive field of force that releases event after event into finite existence (p.49).

This field is then a field of possibility, from which all events arise, and for Pannenberg "a field of possibility . . . is another word for future." Such a conclusion allows him to bring an eschatological perspective into his theology of creation: "every single event as well as the sequence of such events springs contingently from the future of God" (p.49).

We shall conclude with some comments on how Pannenberg views the Incarnation. He argues that the relationship of the Son to the Father is one of unquestioning, spontaneous, unbiased, yet voluntary, subordination. This is the same attitude that Jesus asks of us with regard to God and the coming Kingdom. In taking this attitude we too become sons and daughters of God. Thus the title, Son of God, is inclusive rather than exclusive. All creation is called to accept its subordination to God, though explicitly this occurs only in human beings. In doing so, "human beings do not only realize their particularly human destiny, but they also act in the place of every creature" (p.61). This is possible because Jesus, as Logos, is at work in the whole of creation, but especially in humans made in God's image.

Comments on theological method

In Pannenberg's own terms his work is an introduction to systematic theology. It is systematic in that it seeks to systematically relate a number of key doctrinal areas into a single comprehensive viewpoint. The task of systematic theology is then to start with "God and all things in relation to God." In scope (and in execution, in his three-volume magnum opus, *Systematic Theology*) such a project rivals the vision of Thomas Aquinas who also sought to bring the whole Christian faith within a single systematic viewpoint. In both cases this is not simply a matter of forcing Christian faith into a preexisting philosophical straightjacket. Rather it is a creative, constructive task which enters into a critical dialogue with the philosophical and other resources present in the culture. For Pannenberg these resources include both modern science and modern historical criticism, which were, of course, unavailable to Aquinas.

Truly systematic theologians of such scope are relatively rare in contemporary theology. Generally contemporary theologians are satisfied with historical and descriptive studies of theological issues. As Pannenberg notes, a systematic project almost inevitably requires a willingness to enter into metaphysical issues, and contemporary theologians, apart from those attracted to process thought, are suspicious of the totalizing claims of metaphysics. There is also considerable suspicion of systematic thought itself, as this can also be seen as too totalizing. Still, Pannenberg mounts a spirited defence of the need for both a workable knowledge of metaphysics and a systematic approach.

Given this sharp focus on systematic theology, it is natural to compare Pannenberg's account of the role of systematic theology with Lonergan's functional specialty, systematics. Both conceive of the task in terms of presenting a systematic account, or understanding, of Christian faith. However, Lonergan does not see systematics as increasing the certitude of faith, since the question of truth is settled in the specialty of doctrine. Pannenberg, on the other hand, stresses the fact that the coherence attained in a systematic theology is a criterion for the truth of faith. We can perhaps see a tension in Pannenberg's approach from this. Does systematic theology establish the truth of doctrines through the ultimate criterion of coherence, or does it simply verify, using that same criterion, what faith already knows to be true? If the former, what is the status of those doctrines before being dealt with by systematic theology? If the latter, what does systematic theology really add?

There are still deeper differences in approach here. While Pannenberg rejects the so-called psychological approach of the Western tradition (essentially that of Augustine and Aquinas) to the Trinity, Lonergan sees it as an almost paradigmatic example of what systematic theology is all about. What Pannenberg dismisses as a Platonic intellectualizing of the Christian tradition, Lonergan appreciates as an incipient "turn to the subject" characteristic of much modern thought. Whereas Pannenberg turns to metaphysics, Lonergan grasps in human consciousness the possibility of critically grounding metaphysics, and providing an adequate language for theology. Pannenberg is fearful that such a turn will ultimately lead to subjectivism and a "retreat to commitment," whereas Lonergan claims that the foundations of theology are in conversion, with its religious, moral and intellectual dimensions.

What we see here are two radically different solutions to the difficulties faced by contemporary theology. Can we "turn to the subject," as Lonergan asks, without falling into total subjectivism, as Pannenberg fears? On the other hand, if the task of theology is to give an account of "God and all things in relation to God," is not human subjectivity itself a reality which needs to be integrated into a systematic theology? In this regard Pannenberg's description of a human being as a "self-consciously discerning animal" (p.51) is perhaps less than satisfying, compared with the nuanced accounts of human subjectivity in Augustine and Aquinas. Still one must admire the breadth and scope of Pannenberg's project and its determination to produce a theology which is historically critical and scientifically literate. Few can match him.

DISCUSSION QUESTIONS

• Pannenberg claims that we should take Biblical statements on God's knowledge as metaphorical. Do you agree? What criteria could we use to determine what is, and what is not, metaphorical in the Bible with respect to God?

• Pannenberg is critical of process theology for compromising the transcendence of God. Does his proposal that the Holy Spirit be considered as a field of force pervading creation escape from this same criticism?

Bibliography

As I noted above, Pannenberg has written extensively in theology, touching on areas such as anthropology, spirituality, ecclesiology, ethics, Christology and the relationship between theology and science. I shall mention only some of these below:
Revelation as History, London: Macmillan, 1968—this is a collection of essays by Pannenberg and others which helped establish his reputation. It is a groundbreaking work which challenged accepted accounts of revelation by proposing that revelation is identical with universal history.
Jesus—God and Man, Philadelphia/London: Westminster Press/ SCM Press, 1968—this is a major contribution to Christology. Pannenberg displays a thorough appreciation of biblical, historical and systematic concerns. It has been and remains highly influential.
Basic Questions in Theology, Vols 1–3, Philadelphia/London: Westminster Press/SCM Press, 1970, 1971, 1973—this three-volume set covers a wide variety of theological issues, but not in any systematic manner. They do display the breadth of Pannenberg's concerns.

Systematic Theology, Vols 1–2, Grand Rapids: Eerdmans, 1991, 1994—this is Pannenberg's magnum opus, the culmination of his theological life. This is not a work for beginners, but for the serious student of theology. There is a third volume due soon, though the German original is in print.

For a more comprehensive treatment of Pannenberg's early work the following books are helpful:

A. Galloway, *Wolfhart Pannenberg* in *Contemporary Religious Thinker Series*, London: George Allen and Unwin, 1973.

E.F. Tupper, *The Theology of Wolfhart Pannenberg*, London: SCM Press, 1974.

CHAPTER 9

Karl Rahner, *Transcendental Theology I*

No Catholic theologian has contributed more to the development of contemporary theology than Karl Rahner. He has made major contributions to every area of theology, through his books, articles, theological dictionaries and his multivolume "notebooks," *Theological Investigations*. This contribution has been made despite the difficulty of his style, which even German theologians prefer to read in English translation. A widely-circulated story has it that Karl's brother Hugo, a theologian in his own right, has joked that he must translate Karl into German one day! As with all great creative thinkers, Rahner is forced to take language to its limits in order to express the reality which he has grasped.

Rahner's style of theologizing is called Transcendental, since it draws on the transcendental philosophy of Kant. Rahner was a key figure in the school of thought called Transcendental Thomists, initiated by Joseph Maréchal (1878–1944). Maréchal sought to integrate the thought of Kant with that of Thomas Aquinas. He criticized Kant's epistemology as too static, and as not giving sufficient attention to the process of judgment whereby we judge that such and such is true. He sought to overcome these difficulties through the introduction of a dynamic structure of questioning and answering within the subject, and renewed focus on the process of judgment.

Maréchal argued that every human judgment of truth was an implicit affirmation of the existence of God since it contained an implicit affirmation of the reasonableness of the world. Since it is unreasonable for the world to be reasonable by chance, the world must find its ultimate ground in the reason which is God. In this way, Maréchal went against the Kantian doctrine that it is impossible to prove the existence of God. Sadly, Maréchal had to spend much of his creative energy defending himself from the charge of being a Kantian. Historically, it is important to realize that Kant had been one of the main "adversaries" of Vatican I and its condemnation of Kantian positions were still ringing in Catholic ears.

Inspired by Maréchal, Rahner wrote his doctorate in philosophy, *Spirit in the World*. As with Maréchal's work, this was an attempt to synthesize the work of Aquinas with the critical philosophy of Kant. Rahner was also influenced by the German philosopher, Martin Heidegger, under whom he had studied while a student. His thesis was rejected as too Kantian, though it was circulated privately and was later published. It can still be purchased today. Those who rejected this original work are long forgotten, while Rahner ascended to greater heights! Rahner later completed a doctorate in theology on the Church's origin from the wound in Christ's side, as portrayed in the early Fathers. This led to a lifelong career teaching theology.

Out of this background, Rahner's style of theologizing is thoroughly philosophical. Indeed some would argue that, with Rahner, theology becomes philosophical anthropology. It should also be noted that while Rahner's theology involves a turn to the subject, it is still couched in the language of metaphysics rather than psychology (cf. Sebastian Moore). In that way Rahner needs "unpacking" or translating into more accessible psychological language, unless one is willing to put in the effort to master Rahner's own conceptualization.

For a reader coming out of a Protestant tradition, Rahner's philosophical style could give cause to pause, especially when one considers that his major book, *Foundations of Christian Faith*, contains only a handful of scriptural quotations and references. However, such a philosophical approach is firmly entrenched in Catholic tradition. It is a mark of the power of that tradition that Rahner is able to produce such a profound reflection on Christian faith while making only scant direct reference to Scripture.

Material under consideration—*Foundations of Christian Faith*, New York/London, Crossroad/ Darton, Longman and Todd, 1978

Foundations of Christian Faith: An Introduction to the Idea of Christianity is Rahner's attempt to produce his own *Summa*, a sum total, at a "first level of inquiry," of the Christian faith. *Foundations* is written, as it were, as an introductory text for students beginning their study of theology. It is at a first level of reflection, seeking to lay the foundations for further theological study. As its subtitle states, it is an introduction to the idea of Christianity, dealing with Christianity almost as a theoretical possibility. Some would say that this betrays an Hegelian influence, an idealism, a search for the one encompassing idea which encloses all reality. (Typically, theology students will begin their studies with a course in fundamental theology which deals with such questions as apologetics, grounds for faith, and revelation.)

Rahner wants to be able to "justify" Christian faith, not in the manner of an abstract apologetics, which seeks to justify faith without any reference to its content (a nineteenth-century approach), but to justify it in its totality, a total idea (we can see here the influence of Hegel). The tradition that Rahner is reacting against began with an argument for the necessity of revelation, the credibility of Jesus grounded in his miracles and particularly the resurrection, his founding of the Church with a visible structure and its necessity for salvation. Various dogmas, particularly the central doctrine of the Trinity, were simply part of the content revealed, but are not intrinsically related to the whole process of revelation itself or even to human existence.

Rahner, on the other hand, seeks a justification which will not involve a detailed justification of each part, which would be a complex theological task, or a merely abstract justification which makes no contact with the contents of faith. Rahner wants an overall and foundational justification which points to the credibility of the entire Christian message, one in which the various revealed doctrines are implicitly contained in the justification itself.

Here we can see both similarities with and differences from

the approach of Küng. Küng, too, rejects the abstract apologetics of the nineteenth-century. However his approach is not foundational but critico-historical, an attempt at a relatively detailed historical justification of central elements of the Christian tradition. Rahner, on the other hand, uses his own powerful anthropology to foreshadow the whole content of the Christian faith. Consequently, it is not difficult to see vastly different styles of theology in the two authors.

A key concern here is "intellectual honesty"—can I be intellectually honest in my Christian faith? The type of justification Rahner seeks would allow me to be intellectually honest without going into the type of detailed justification that only a specialist can attain. Rahner sees such a process of justification as necessary because the person coming to theology today "does not feel secure in a faith which is taken for granted and is supported by a homogeneous religious milieu common to everyone" (p.5). What needs to be justified is why we should risk life in faith in Jesus as the crucified and raised God-man.

A key method in this process of justification is the "transcendental deduction" (refer to Kant). As it is such a central process in Rahner's theological method, we shall now spend some time in examining it. (At this stage, it might be of advantage to reread the material on Kant in Chapter 2.)

A transcendental deduction begins with the question "what are the *a priori* conditions for the possibility of . . . ?" and seeks answers in the transcendental (*a priori* or given) structures of the subject. A key example of such a structure is questioning. Questioning is a given structure of human subjectivity. One cannot, as Rahner says, question the question. To do so is to invoke the very structure under analysis. Moreover, questioning is the *a priori* condition for the possibility of knowing something. Without questions, there are no answers!

The aim of such a deduction is to arrive at a "correlation," i.e. it is an attempt to correlate the Christian message with these transcendental structures of human subjectivity:

> If moreover, the horizon of human existence which grounds and encompasses all human knowledge is a mystery, and it is, then man has a positive affinity, given at least with grace, to those

Christian mysteries which constitute the basic content of faith (p.12).

Here we see the swing between object and subject, between the objective horizon of human existence and the subjectivity of human knowledge, between the objective Christian mysteries and the subjective "positive affinity" given in grace to those mysteries. The transcendental deduction seeks to uncover these "positive affinities" and so provide a transcendental anticipation of those mysteries.

Rahner describes the process of the transcendental deduction as follows:

> [T]he structure of the subject itself is an "a priori," that is, it forms an antecedent law governing what and how something can become manifest to the knowing subject. . . . This in no way implies that the realities which present themselves cannot manifest themselves as they really are. A keyhole forms an "a priori" law governing what key fits in, *but it thereby discloses something about the key itself* (p.19) (emphasis added).

Hence, Rahner begins his investigation with the typically Kantian question: "What kind of a hearer does Christianity anticipate so that its real and ultimate message can even be heard?" (p.24)—what does the object reveal about the subject and vice versa? Here the key is the Christian message, the keyhole the human person. Our knowledge of the human person allows us to anticipate the Christian message. It is the correlation between this anticipated message and the actual message of the Christian faith which provides Rahner with his required justification for Christianity.

Using this transcendental method, Rahner investigates the human person as person and subject, as transcendent being, as shown in the transcendental structures of knowing and freedom. For Rahner, unlike Kant, knowledge puts us in touch with being, with reality. Further, freedom is not unknowable but an irreducible datum of human existence, something which, like the question, we affirm even in the act of freely denying. These two transcendental structures show us to be "pure openness for absolutely everything, for being as such" (p.22).

It is human freedom which constitutes us as responsible subjects. For Rahner freedom is "always mediated by the concrete reality of time and space, of man's materiality and his history" (p.36). Rahner distinguishes between freedom in its origin, or transcendental freedom, and freedom which "enters into and is mediated to itself by the medium of the world" (p.37), a categorial freedom. Thus a person in prison has transcendental freedom though his or her categorical freedom may be severely impaired. However, Rahner insists that these are not two freedoms but two moments which form the single unity of human freedom. This gives us the two main categories in Rahner's thought—the transcendental and the historical (or categorical).

Human freedom raises the question of salvation as the "final and definitive validity of a person's true self-understanding and true self-realization in freedom before God" (p.39). The working out of freedom and salvation is in history, since the human person is historical by nature. "Transcendentality and freedom are realized in history" (p.40).

Some have argued that Rahner's transcendental approach is rationalistic, i.e. it tries to deduce the mysteries of faith simply by the use of reason. This is not really accurate. It is more important to note the circularity of the argument. In fact, our concrete knowledge of the human subject is already conditioned by our knowledge of the Christian message. However, this knowledge of the human subject, whatever its source, can be further verified by human experience and hence has an independence from that source. The circle is not vicious, more a spiral of learning. This circularity is a further example of how subject and object mutually condition each other.

Moreover, Rahner argues that it is not simply that our knowledge of the Christian message conditions our knowledge of the human subject, but that the reality of the Christian message conditions the reality of the human subject, that the human subject exists with a radical orientation to God. It is this orientation or "supernatural existential" which marks the human person out as a potential "hearer of the word" (the title of one of Rahner's early works). It is this supernatural existential, which is already a share in God's grace or divine self-communication, which allows us to hear the Word of God, which is God, as a truly divine Word, and not reduce it to a merely human word.

Here we see Rahner pulling out of his anthropology key theological themes of Trinity (grace as Holy Spirit, Word of God as divine) and Incarnation (the Word of God becomes human without being merely human), as a correlation to the supernatural existential of the subject. For Rahner, the mysteries of the Trinity, Incarnation and grace are not three distinct mysteries, but all aspects of the one mystery of the divine self-communication.

Indeed, the concept of divine self-communication is central to Rahner's theology. For Rahner, God communicates God's own being, through God's Word, who enters into human history, and through God's Spirit, who transforms human subjectivity so that it may receive and rejoice in the Word. Through this act of self-communication, God reveals Godself to us as a Trinitarian God. The very structure of revelation, in Word and Spirit, speaks of God's Trinitarian nature. Thus, the Trinity is not simply some extrinsic content of revelation, but is part of the structure of revelation itself.

Note also that Rahner's approach to Trinity here closely follows that of Karl Barth (see Chapter 4). It is also not difficult to make contacts between Rahner's notion of a supernatural existential and Moore's psychological analysis of the human person radically oriented to God who is ultimate source of all affirmation.

One of the problems that this analysis of the human person raises is the question of the relationship between grace and nature. For Rahner:

> . . . the spiritual creature is constituted **to begin with** as the possible addressee of such a divine self-communication . . . . **In the only order which is real**, the emptiness of the transcendental creature exists *because* the fullness of God creates the emptiness *in order* to communicate himself to it (p.123) (bold emphasis added).

On this understanding, the pure state of nature is just a theoretical construct, something which exists as a possibility, but about which we can only speculate and of which we have no experience. In the only order which is real, the concrete order of creation, we exist from the beginning with an emptiness that only God can fill. In the only order which is real, the whole of creation is radically oriented towards its completion in Christ. Hence Rahner develops a "Christology within an evolutionary view of the world" (p.178ff).

Such a Christology does not see the world as a static reality but as a dynamic, evolving process. In that process, matter continually seeks to express itself in ever higher, more complex forms. In this process, spirit is not something superimposed upon matter from above, but is matter become conscious of itself and the cosmos. Thus, the evolution of humankind from the material universe marks a high point in a dynamic which is part of the nature of matter itself.

To explore this process of complexification, Rahner introduces the notion of "active self-transcendence." He produces a metaphysical analysis of how a finite being can "become" something more than it originally is, can transcend its own reality and "leap" to a higher state. For Rahner, such self-transcendence can only be understood "as taking place by the power of the absolute fullness of being [God]" (p.185). Thus, evolution does not remove God from creation but places God at the heart of creation.

In such a framework, the Incarnation is not to be viewed simply as God reaching down to humankind from above, but also as the realization of the inner dynamic towards self-transcendence implicit in the evolutionary process. In Jesus, the self-transcendence of the human spirit reaches its ultimate fulfillment and breaks through into the divine. Again this should not be seen as an "achievement" of Jesus, in some adoptive sense, but as God's definitive self-communication in Jesus. Creation as a whole is seen by Rahner as a deficient mode of God's self-communication which then reaches perfection in the Incarnation.

This analysis of the Incarnation, as a culmination of an evolutionary process, again illustrates Rahner's transcendental method. The objective process of evolution through active self-transcendence finds its subjective counterpart in the conscious self-transcendence of the subject in knowing and loving. Central to the transcendental method is the notion of a "structural isomorphism" between the dynamic processes of consciousness and the structures of material reality, or, as Rahner would say, the "keyhole" of human consciousness already discloses something about the "key" of the material world. Lonergan exploits this more fully in his notion of emergent probability (see Lonergan's *Insight*, Chapter 4).

The above brief outline does not pretend to cover all the material in this profound and difficult book. That is not my aim. My aim is to help open up the material by an examination of its themes and method so that others may enter Rahner's work forewarned and forearmed. To that extent the above is little more than an invitation.

Comments on theological method

In a sense, much of what we have been speaking about already has been related to Rahner's method. In a sense, again, the method is the theology. To grasp the method is to have an approach to any and all theological questions. It is the open-ended, heuristic nature of Rahner's method which indicates its powerfully foundational value, in the terms given in Chapter 4. Rahner's foundation is the human subject grasped in the light of his or her religious, moral and intellectual potentialities.

It is the foundational nature of this work which leads to the abstract level of its treatment of Christianity. Much of the discussion could have been carried on even if there was no Incarnation of Jesus Christ, no historical person of Jesus at all. Rahner is seeking the "heuristic structures" which he judges make Christianity intelligible—it is an anticipatory Christology, soteriology and ecclesiology which finds its proper response in the historical Jesus and the founding of the Church.

One difficulty that people often have with Rahner is his metaphysical approach to theology. Rahner's theology rests on a complex metaphysical theory which is really only made explicit in his doctoral work *Spirit in the World*. As is often the case, such a complex metaphysical system will stand or fall with the authority of the person who creates it. While Rahner's metaphysics has roots in Aristotelian-Thomistic metaphysics, it is still uniquely his own. Many would want a more critical basis for adopting such an approach.

Others would judge his approach too abstract, though, as Rahner states, this is simply a foundational course and not meant to be too specific. It is this abstract nature of Rahner's reflections which have led to criticism from one of his outstanding pupils, Johann Baptist Metz. For Metz, the transcendental method of Rahner runs the risk of reducing history to historicity, i.e. history is not considered in its concrete reality but simply as a category of human existence. Thus, Rahner will often speak about the historical conditioning of the human person without delving into the precise effect of this conditioning in our present historical circumstances. Metz fears that this acts in such a way as to implicitly support the status quo. However, as Metz says, even when criticizing Rahner, one has much to learn from him.

DISCUSSION QUESTIONS

- What implications do you see the theory of evolution having for Christian faith, for Christology?

- What relationships do you see between Christian faith in God as Trinity and a Christian understanding of revelation?

Bibliography

Rahner's own works are too numerous to list. Perhaps his most significant contribution lies in his *Theological Investigations*, Vols 1–23, New York/London, Crossroad/Darton, Longman and Todd, collections of essays on every conceivable theological subject. He has also made significant contributions to the theological encyclopedia, *Sacramentum Mundi*, London: Burns and Oates, 1968-70, which he edited.

Fortunately there are some good introductions to Rahner's thought.

L. Roberts, *The Achievement of Karl Rahner*, New York: Herder and Herder, 1967.

G. Vass, *A Theologian in Search of a Philosophy: Understanding Karl Rahner*, London: Sheed and Ward, 1985.

The Mystery of Man and the Foundations of a Theological System: Understanding Karl Rahner, London: Sheed and Ward, 1985.
W. Dych, *Karl Rahner*, London: Geoffrey Chapman, 1992.

Also of value is the recent collection of texts with commentary drawn from Rahner's writings:
G. Kelly, *Karl Rahner: Theologian of the Graced Search for Meaning*, Minneapolis: Fortress Press, 1992.

CHAPTER 10

Bernard Lonergan,
Transcendental Theology II

As with Karl Rahner, Lonergan has been identified with the theological movement known as Transcendental Thomism. Lonergan's first two major works were in fact directed towards an interpretation of the work of Aquinas, basically as historical studies attempting to retrieve the past. The first, Lonergan's doctoral thesis, published as *Grace and Freedom*, studied the thought of Aquinas on questions of grace, human freedom and divine providence. Lonergan quickly rejected the two standard interpretations given within Catholic theology as inadequate and set out to recover what he saw as the authentic position of Aquinas on these questions.

His next major study, published as *Verbum, Word and Idea in Aquinas*, attempted a similar recovery of Aquinas on the Trinity. It was in this study that Lonergan developed the philosophical approach which was to dominate his whole life's work. Out of the conclusions of this study came *Insight*, Lonergan's philosophical magnum opus. Its starting point was not metaphysics but cognitional theory, Kant's starting point; Lonergan's conclusion was metaphysics, essentially Thomistic in structure, hence the label Transcendental Thomism.

Even from his first study, Lonergan had his mind set on the question of theological method. In the unpublished preface of his doctoral thesis, Lonergan already bemoaned the lack of any precise method for resolving disputes in "speculative theology." For Lonergan, method always remained a central concern. *Insight*, a work of over seven hundred pages, was written simply as a preface to a further work on theological method. Though *Insight* was published in 1957, the further work on method did not appear until 1972 with the publication of *Method in Theology*. The only other substantial English works available are collections of essays, *Collection*, *Second Collection* and *A Third Collection*. Now that Lonergan has died, it is hoped that various Latin works will appear in translation. Indeed at present the University of Toronto Press is publishing several volumes of the *Collected Works of Bernard Lonergan*, which will eventually include English translations of previously untranslated Latin works.

The last years of his life were spent on the study of economics. Lonergan had developed his own macroeconomic theory in the 1930s as a response to the upheavals of the Depression. However, its dynamic "circulation analysis" was ahead of its time, so Lonergan shelved it for his theological and philosophical endeavors. After the publication of *Method in Theology*, he resumed his interest in economics partly as a response to the demands for sound economic models issued by Liberation theologians. This illustrates the strength of his conviction of the necessity of dialoguing with contemporary culture.

When reading Lonergan's writings, one is quickly aware that one is in the presence of a great mind. There is a mixture of clarity and profundity which is the mark of a true genius. Lonergan was the contemporary Renaissance person who was equally at home discussing mathematics, quantum mechanics, philosophy, theology, history, economics or psychology. While many recent theologians recognize a debt to Lonergan (e.g. D. Tracy, M. Lamb, S. Moore, P. Chirico, L. Orsy, to name a few), his work is still to reach its full impact. (His influence lies mainly in North America. European theologians, on the other hand, remain suspicious of anything non-European.) In many ways, he is a philosopher's philosopher and a theologian's theologian. His works will never be "popular," though his influence has been widespread.

Material under consideration—*A Third Collection*, New York/London: Paulist Press/Geoffrey Chapman, 1985

A Third Collection, as the name implies, is simply a collection of papers written and delivered in a variety of situations. They touch on a large number of diverse topics, from concern with authority ("Dialectic of Authority") to a "Post-Hegelian Philosophy of Religion," to John XXIII's intention in calling Vatican II. One can grasp from these the broad sweep of Lonergan's interests. Few of these essays, however, are directly theological in the sense of dealing with classical theological topics of grace, sin, God, Jesus. Generally, they deal with theology from a position once removed. They deal with method, with the relationship between theology and tradition, with culture. However, we do have one essay dealing directly with theological matter, "Christology Today: Methodological Reflections," and it is on this that we shall focus.

"Christology Today" is Lonergan's response to some theological proposals put by Piet Schoonenberg, an eminent Dutch theologian and educator, concerning the nature and person of Jesus in relation to the Council of Chalcedon. The Council held that in Jesus Christ there are two natures, human and divine, within one person of Christ. Later Councils taught that the one person of Christ is divine, the second person of the Trinity. This teaching of the Council became the key dogmatic expression of the Church concerning the Incarnation.

Schoonenberg is objecting to what is called a Christology from above, which he claims this Council represents. Such a Christology is presented in the prologue of John's Gospel which speaks of a pre-existent Word of God which descends from heaven to take on our human nature. Schoonenberg, on the other hand, wants to initiate a Christology from below, which starts with the humanity of Jesus and sees Jesus as one especially chosen by God. Such an approach can be found in the Synoptic Gospels. In such an ascending Christology, one would ultimately conclude with the divinity of Jesus, but one would not use that divinity as explanatory of anything about Jesus.

As part of his proposal, Schoonenberg wants to be able to

say that not only is Jesus human, but that Jesus is a human person. Such a position would seem on the surface to contradict the logic of Chalcedon and the terminology of later Councils which spoke of Jesus as a divine person. The question is whether such a position contradicts not only the logic and terminology, but also the intention of the Councils. Ultimately this raises the question of the distinction between person and nature and it is this that Lonergan seeks to address.

Lonergan proceeds via a number of prolegomena, or preliminary suggestions, which might facilitate a later synthesis. In psychology he notes the possibility, not only of development from below up, but also from above down, not only nothing loved unless known, but also, not truly known unless loved. This is the same twofold ascending and descending motion we have seen operative in Lonergan's method discussed in Chapter 4.

In philosophy he notes the distinction between the world of immediacy (the world of immediate sensory experience, of the newborn child) and the human world mediated by meaning. Moreover, within the world mediated by meaning it is common to argue not only from below up, but from above down, not only from the *causa cognoscendi* (the cause of knowledge) but also from the *causa essendi* (the cause of being). Thus we may argue from our knowledge of the phases of the moon to the fact that the moon is a sphere (from knowledge to being). Alternatively, we can argue that the reason we see phases of the moon is that the moon is a sphere (from being to knowledge).

Lonergan uses these two observations to challenge Schoonenberg's contention that we should not use the divinity of Jesus as explanatory but simply come to it as a conclusion.

In history he notes the shift from history as belief to history as science and the impact this has on New Testament studies. Scripture is now seen not so much as a diary of the events in Jesus' life, as a statement of the belief of the early Church communities. In discussing the New Testament as history it is important to distinguish between different types of history. Here we can see the outlines of Lonergan's method as given in Chapter 4:

The textual critic can specialize in the manuscript tradition [research]. The exegete can master all related literatures and bring them to bear on an understanding of this or that section of text [interpretation]. The factual historian can assemble the factual statements in the New Testament, submit them to his critical scrutiny, and seek to fit them in the context of other known contemporary events [history]. The ethically oriented historian can compare the moral attitudes of New Testament personages with those of other human communities or he can subsume them under some moral code to praise or blame them [dialectics]. But while all of these approaches have their significance and value, none of them deals with what manifestly is the principal concern of the New Testament. For first and last, the New Testament is a book with a message . . . (p.83).

It is the message quality of the New Testament, with its counterpart in conversion which allows Lonergan to raise Christology as a religious, and not just historical, question. The New Testament texts are not a "telling of the facts" or a process of "passing moral judgments on past figures." They are kerygma, salvation history, and hence intensely personal, standing as an objective pole to a personal subjective response of conversion.

By making these distinctions between the different levels of questioning, Lonergan overcomes the commonly-drawn distinction between the Jesus of history and the Christ of faith. The factual and moral historian asks specific questions about the one reality, Jesus of Nazareth. The person of faith approaches the same reality, but asking a different type of question. The distinction is not between the Jesus of history and the Christ of faith, but between the questions we address to the one reality, Jesus Christ. Thus:

. . . this radical opposition [between the Jesus of history and the Christ of faith] tends to vanish when (1) religious people correct their pre-critical views of history and (2) learned people come to recognize in the New Testament contemporary and so firsthand evidence on the beliefs of the early Church (p.86).

Thus, the historical investigation of the Gospels when raised to an existential level raises a theological question—how are we to understand this person, Jesus of Nazareth? Who is his man, that even the winds and seas obey? In order to investigate this question, Lonergan develops a heuristic structure, a "conjunction both of data on the side of the object and of an operative criterion on the side of the subject" (p. 87). In Christology the object is Jesus, while the data we have on him is found in the New Testament witness of the faith of the early Church. On the side of the subject there is the Holy Spirit, given to us by the Father, making us sons and daughters of God and enabling us to acknowledge Jesus as Lord.

We can see Lonergan's transcendental methodology at work here, with subject and object mutually conditioning one another. The interior gift of the Holy Spirit both makes meaningful and is made meaningful by the Incarnation of the Word of God in the person of Jesus Christ. Without the gift of the Spirit, the Word could not be heard. Without the coming of the Word, the interior presence of the Spirit never meets its proper object.

Part of the New Testament data about this Word incarnate is the repeated use of the title "Son of God" in relation to Jesus. It is this, states Lonergan, which:

> . . . gives rise to the multiple question: How are we in our minds
> to understand Jesus as the Son of God? Are we to suppose it is
> a mythic or merely honorific title such as was given to kings?
> Or does it simply denote the mission of the Messiah? Or does it
> point to an inner reality such as is our own divine sonship
> through Christ and in the Spirit, so that as God in us is the Spirit,
> so God in Jesus is the Word? Or does the sonship of Jesus mean,
> as the church for centuries has understood it, that Jesus was truly
> man leading a truly human life but his identity was the identity
> of the eternal Son of God consubstantial with the Father? (p.88)

In this context, Lonergan sees the Council of Chalcedon, not simply as proposing a heuristic model (one person, two natures), but positing it as true. What lies at the heart of this is an understanding of the role of dogma in general, where dogma is seen not simply to be adding new interpretations, or making statements bound by particular cultures and time, but as getting to the heart of an issue and making a judgment of truth about it. As Lonergan notes, this position is not popular among contemporary theologians. There is no shortage of those who consider dogmas meaningless or simply do not advert to the notion of dogma at all. I have already noted that I see the area of dogma as a central problem for contemporary theology.

Moving on from these dogmatic considerations, Lonergan seeks to systematically ground the distinction between person and nature. However, rather than use the terms, "person" and "nature," he uses the terms "subject" and "subjectivity" as more in keeping with contemporary philosophical language. He then investigates the distinction between the unity within subjectivity and the unity of subject. While my consciousness is one, it is clearly developing, changing. My subjectivity now is different from that when I was a child, not only in terms of content but also in terms of the potentialities that have been developed. However, I am the same person, the same subject, I am me and not John Doe! On the one hand, there is the unity of intelligible relations, the subjectivity which makes me what I am here and now. On the other hand, there is the one-and-the-same unity which distinguishes me from another. Lonergan concludes that there is a distinction between subject and subjectivity, between person and nature, so that Jesus can be a divine subject but still have a human subjectivity, be a divine person and still have a human nature. Lonergan also discusses the divine subjectivity proper to the divine subject in terms of a psychological analogy of the Trinity. However, this would take us too far afield. For the basic Christological issue at hand, it is important to note that these two subjectivities exist "without modification or confusion."

In all this, Lonergan is displaying "conservative" theological tendencies—a desire to defend the teachings of Church Councils and to defend the notion of dogma. However, there is no naivete in his approach. It is based on a critical appropriation of the past, combined with the best of contemporary scholarship. It is also significant to note that what is achieved is basically a "translation" of Chalcedon into contemporary terms. Rather than person and nature, Lonergan speaks of subject and subjectivity. However, the mystery as to how one subject can be constituted through two distinct subjectivities remains.

It would be wrong to simply label Lonergan as a conservative. While theologically he upholds traditional formulations, the sweep of his thought as a whole is far from conservative. If we consider the two essays which "bracket" the one we have considered, "Prolegomena to the Study of the Emerging Religious Consciousness of Our Time" and "Healing and Creating in History," we find quite radical critiques of bureaucracies (as a major source of human alienation), of transnational corporations (a critique of the maxim of maximizing profit), as well as evidence of universalist religious tendencies focusing on religious experience as a common point of all religions. Here a quite "conservative" theological position is married to quite radical social and cultural critiques, which extend their criticism even to the life of the Church.

Comments on theological method

As one might expect, Lonergan's theology follows the theological method which he developed and which I outlined in Chapter 4. Indeed, the essay we have considered is concerned with "methodological reflections." This use of his "method" is most clearly seen in the historical prolegomena where Lonergan distinguishes between the different levels of activity undertaken in historical research.

Lonergan distinguishes between the textual, interpretative, factual and moral aspects of the historian's work. These correspond to the imperatives: be attentive, be intelligent, be reasonable and be responsible, and to the upward movement of research, interpretation, history and dialectics. In a sense, Lonergan is here adopting Schoonenberg's ascending approach. The divinity of Jesus is not evident at the level of factual or moral history. However, Lonergan is arguing that there is a dynamism operating within us which moves us beyond these levels, which calls for a conversion and which leads to an affirmation of the divinity of Jesus. Already this affirmation is part of the descending phase since it comes out of conversion, the gift of the Spirit making us sons and daughters of God.

From this perspective, a purely ascending Christology will not really be able to arrive at an affirmation of the divinity of

Jesus. Indeed, this is Lonergan's fear with Schoonenberg's purely ascending approach. Lonergan claims that Schoonenberg's position that Jesus is not just human, but also a human person, ends up with Jesus as "just a man" and nothing else.

The descending phase in Lonergan's theology is seen in his commitment to the doctrine of Chalcedon, in his attempts to systematically understand the Incarnation by relating it to the mystery of the Trinity through a psychological analogy, and in his use of the categories of subject and subjectivity as more appropriate in communicating the intent of the doctrine than the categories of person and nature.

Perhaps in this essay we can see Lonergan's commitment to analyzing theological method bearing fruit. By clarifying the distinctions between different types of history, by his psychological and philosophical observation, he is able to focus on what are the central issues and pursue them with single-minded and methodical determination.

DISCUSSION QUESTIONS

- What difference, if any, do you see between a theological reinterpretation or translation of a dogma and a new scientific theory reinterpreting empirical data?

- On the basis of the account above, how would you understand the difference between the approach of Lonergan and the approach of Schoonenberg with regard to the dogma of Chalcedon?

Bibliography

Lonergan has not been a prolific writer of books, though he has had collections of essays published, such as the one we have considered. The most readily available works are as follows:
Insight, New York: Longmans, revised, 1958—Lonergan's philosophical magnum opus. This densely argued work of seven hundred pages is a philosophical classic. Many are put off by its scientific and mathematical examples given in the first few

chapters. However, it rewards the effort of perseverance.

Understanding and Being, New York: Edwin Mellen Press, 1980—this is a sort of *"Insight* for beginners" book. It is an edited version of adult education lectures given by Lonergan on the material in *Insight*.

Method in Theology, New York: Seabury Press, 1972; London: Darton, Longman and Todd, 1974—in this work, Lonergan not only develops his theological method as prefigured in *Insight*, he also develops new positions which go beyond those found in *Insight*. It is more readable than *Insight* but still in fairly dense, telegraphic form.

The reader should also consider the works *Collection*, New York: Herder and Herder, 1967, and *A Second Collection*, Philadelphia/London: Westminster Press/Darton, Longman and Todd, 1974. These works, which, together with *A Third Collection*, span a career of over forty years, give a clear indication of both the continuity and the development in Lonergan's thought.

For a more detailed analysis of Lonergan's work see:

D. Tracy, *The Achievement of Bernard Lonergan*, New York: Herder and Herder, 1970.

F. Crowe, *The Lonergan Enterprise*, Cambridge: Cowley, 1980.

Lonergan, London: Geoffrey Chapman, 1992.

R. Liddy, *Transforming Light: Intellectual Conversion in the Early Lonergan*, Collegeville: Michael Glazier, 1993.

CHAPTER 11

Johann Baptist Metz, *Political Theology*

Johann Baptist Metz was a student of Karl Rahner and is a leading figure in the area known as Political Theology. While he shares something of Rahner's transcendental methodology, he has also been a critic of Rahner's approach, in particular claiming that Rahner has not paid sufficient attention to the political dimension of theology. Like Rahner, his style of writing is dense and difficult to get into. Metz's work is definitely not for the novice, though it is still a significant contribution to contemporary theology. Developments in both Liberation Theology and Feminist Theology owe much to the area of Political Theology.

We should begin by clarifying what is meant by the term Political Theology. The term "political" is not used in the narrow sense of political parties, but in the broader, original sense of the *polis*, society as a whole, its governance, its culture, its economy. Political Theology is a theology of the *polis*, a theology which examines social structures, cultural movements, economic philosophies in the penetrating light of the Gospel. While this may have implications in the narrower political sense, its overall vision is broader and more profound.

As I mentioned above, Metz's Political Theology has been an influence on Liberation Theology, but it has also, in its turn, been influenced by Liberation Theology. Metz's original attempts at a Political Theology were more "optimistic," e.g. they gave a positive analysis of the process of secularization. Secularization, the process whereby various spheres of human activity, such as government and legal systems, were moved out of the "divine" sphere and into the human or secular sphere, was seen as liberative of human freedom and hence as being in accord with the dynamism of the Gospel. His later writings, however, have been more influenced by a "hermeneutics of suspicion," by the negative dialectics of the Frankfurt school, and a new appreciation of the role of apocalyptic. The earlier optimism has been replaced by a more serious appreciation of the darker forces operating in present human history.

Political Theology has not attracted as much popular attention or ecclesiastical opposition as has Liberation Theology. Perhaps this is because of its largely German origins, with their ponderous prose. It has, however, given rise to some opposition. Metz, Rahner and the newly-appointed Cardinal Joseph Ratzinger had a public squabble over the denial of a suitable teaching position to Metz. Teaching positions in Catholic Theology in German universities are governed by a concordat with the Vatican. Metz had applied for a position and was rejected by Ratzinger as unsuitable. Rahner then published an open letter to Ratzinger complaining about the treatment of Metz. However, there has been no major ecclesiastical response to Political Theology as there has been to Liberation Theology.

Political Theology is not just a new subject to be added to the theological curriculum. It raises questions about the whole theological project. It constitutes a new theological paradigm, a new way of doing theology. As yet, the ramifications of this paradigm have not been fully felt.

Work under consideration—*Faith in History and Society*, New York/London: The Seabury Press/ Burns & Oates, 1980

Given the difficulty of Metz's work, I shall present a sample of the main themes of his book, *Faith in History and Society— Towards a Practical Fundamental Theology*. This is his most recent work to date on Political Theology and represents his most mature thinking on the subject.

An initial observation can be made from the subtitle of the book—*Towards a Practical Fundamental Theology*. Like Rahner,

Metz is seeking a fundamental theology, a justification for Christianity. For Rahner, this can be achieved in a purely theoretical way, through consideration of the transcendental structures of the human subject—the human subject as hearer of the word. Metz, on the other hand, claims that Christianity cannot be justified in a purely theoretical way, but is primarily justified in its praxis, its committed responsible action. Human persons are not just hearers of the word (cf. the title of one of Rahner's seminal works), but also doers of the word.

The danger of a purely speculative defence of Christian faith is that in its attempt at an ever more comprehensive system of thought (recall here the work of Hegel), it might fall into a "speculative regression into infinity"! It is this type of speculative danger that Metz senses in the work of Rahner, for instance. To avoid such a speculative regression, Metz argues, theology must turn to the concrete subject and the praxis of subjects (p.7).

Hence Metz is interested in a practical fundamental theology. Being practical, such a theology is concerned not only with its theoretical base but also with the practical conditions of its own performance, the ecclesial and social structures which condition its work. Metz seeks to develop a theology which is not naive of its political significance. Thus, Metz asks "who should do theology and where, in whose interests and for whom?" (pp.58–59). All human activities have a political dimension. Metz argues that classical approaches to theology, by ignoring this dimension, have in fact been agents for propping up the status quo.

To illustrate this, we may consider the following. To ask about doing the word is to ask about the structures of human freedom. Such structures, however, are not simply transcendental, a given part of human nature, but are also historical and political in nature. The freedoms of the middle class in Europe or America are not the freedoms of peasants in China. Moreover, the exercise of human freedom is not a private moral concern but also a political act, as, for example, when a Pole goes to Mass in Poland. It is this dimension that Metz insists we never lose sight of.

One of the main themes of Political Theology is that of ideology critique. An ideology is a system of thought that appears so obvious to the holder that judgments of value are presented as empirical facts, that social phenomena are seen as natural, and the interests of the few are obviously those of the whole— what is good for General Motors is good for the USA! Metz identifies some key ideologies which exist within Western society and subjects them to critique. This entails a hermeneutics of suspicion which seeks to uncover the hidden values, the special interests which justify the suffering of the victims of ideological systems by recourse to ideologies which render their suffering "invisible."

Evolutionary thought

One ideology which Metz criticizes is "evolutionary thought." He notes that evolution has become a total account of the universe. Not only life but society, culture, even the Church is said to be evolving. While evolutionary thought has been significant in helping us recognize and appreciate change, it does so by locating the source of change in an impersonal and irresistible "Evolution" and not in human decision-making. In doing so, it robs subjects of their motivation to act. Everything is subsumed into a larger and impersonal "evolutionary movement." The result is apathy:

> Man is at the mercy of a darkly speckled universe and enclosed in an endless continuum of time that is no longer capable of surprising him. He feels that he is caught up in the waves of an anonymous process of evolution sweeping pitilessly over everyone. A new culture of apathy and lack of feeling is being prepared for him in view of his experience of fragile identity (p.6).

What is needed to overcome this is an appreciation of the human person, not as an object of impersonal evolution, but as the subject of human history. Human beings make history through their responsible (or irresponsible) decisions. To invoke evolution is to mask the reality of human agency. Once masked, it is no longer subject to scrutiny, since who can oppose "evolution"? Such a masking can serve only those who are making important decisions about the direction of human social change but are happy to not have their decisions scrutinized. Such a situation pertained in the proponents of "social Darwinism" who transposed the "survival of the fittest" into the social context, to the detriment of the poor and weak.

Metz uses his critique of evolutionary thought to reevaluate the role of apocalyptic in Christian eschatology (pp.177ff). He argues that evolutionary thought has defused the power of Christian eschatology by attempting to make it "non-problematic." Under evolutionary thought, the end-time is simply the culmination of the evolutionary process, a smooth transition into a final perfect state. The eschaton, i.e. the culmination of human history, does not require from me any commitment, any decision, it just happens.

Metz argues that theology, under the influence of evolutionary thought, has been caught in the alternatives of an immanentist or a futurist eschatology, of the "already-now" and the "not-yet." A futurist eschatology sees the end as indefinitely postponed and as unrelated to history. The only hope it offers is for an otherworldly heaven, which I can enter if I behave myself and don't rock the boat—it is, as Marx said, the opiate of the people. An immanentist eschatology, on the other hand, focuses on the present ecstatic experience of God or the Spirit (e.g. Pentecostal movements) and so deflects me from my present historical situation—it is, in a sense, the cocaine of the people! Both these alternatives fail to take history, particularly the historical struggle for justice, seriously. For both, history is endlessly open to revision so that the urgency for change is never acutely felt.

For Metz, an apocalyptic eschatology is one which takes such a struggle seriously. It does not ask: "How much we have already been saved and to what extent we have not yet been saved"? Rather, it asks: "How much time do we (still) have?" (p.177). Apocalyptic eschatology takes seriously the possibility of an end to time, an end to history. How much longer must the poor suffer, how much longer injustice and persecution? The sufferings of the victims of our ideologies cry out to God for justice. An apocalyptic eschatology takes evil and the historical struggle against evil seriously, in a way that evolutionary thought never can.

As an aside, it is important to note that Metz's criticism of evolutionary thought is in no way taking a stance on the evo-lution-creationism debate. The biological theory of evolution, as a scientific theory, is quite distinct from the ideological consid-erations that Metz is examining.

Consumerism

Within the ideology of consumerism, only those things which have "exchange value" within the marketplace are considered to be of social significance. That which has no exchange value is relegated to the private sphere, e.g. values. Religion thus becomes privatized, reduced to the role of celebrating middle-class religious festivals and maintaining private morality. (One might note the German context here, though similar comments could be made about France and Britain.)

> All other values, which may have had a decisive effect on society in the past, but which no longer directly contribute to the func-tioning of the modern middle-class society of exchange have receded into the sphere of the private, individual freedom (p.35).

According to Metz, these ideologies create the "middle-class subject." Such a subject is characterized by two features. He or she enjoys a privatized religion, one which provides a sphere of warmth in a cold and hostile world. Such a religion no longer locates me within a social context, no longer has social meaning. It simply serves as a bolster to my privatized individualism. Secondly, such a subject can see no publicly identifiable role for tradition. Values are identified not by appeal to long-standing tradition, but by reference to public opinion. In this way, the middle-class subject can no longer appeal to tradition as a prin-ciple by which to criticize the present. Such a subject recognizes only the authority of a calculating reason, not the authority of a tradition born of suffering. This is the "concrete human subject" that theology has to deal with, not just the abstract "spirit in the world" of Rahner's transcendental theology.

Here we can see the basis of Metz's criticism of Rahner's transcendental theology. While Rahner's theology aims at a "turn to the subject," Metz claims that this turn is still to an idealised subject, not the more concrete "middle-class subject" of present society. To theologize is not simply to take such a subject for granted, as non-problematic, but also to criticize that subject in the light of the Gospel message. For Metz, the middle-class subject has subverted a Christian understanding of freedom and action:

> . . . a middle-class concept of praxis has to a great extent replaced the authentically Christian concept of freedom and praxis that is critical of society. . . . (I)t has reduced the Christian concept to the level of the private subject existing without problems in society and to that of individual moral righteousness (p.28).

Thus, for a subject who does not recognize the value of tradition, Metz puts forward the notion of dogmas as subversive memories of freedom, subversive of the ideologies which seek to limit the exercise of human freedom. For the subject who recognizes only the authority of competence, Metz considers the authority of Jesus which does not derive from his "competence," but which is rather the authority of suffering. It is the memory of this suffering (*memoria passionis*) which is central to Christian tradition, recalled at every Eucharist. The middle-class subject is challenged to recognize the authority of Jesus' suffering and the tradition which keeps that memory alive.

For Metz, it is the memory of the suffering, death and resurrection of Jesus which is the hope and promise of a future for all those who have died, who have become the forgotten victims of social ideologies which have justified the victors over the victims. The gospel narratives contain subversive memories of Jesus, of his mission, of his dangerous freedom to reach out to outcasts. Such memories are kept alive in narratives, the stories of the victims, whose telling and retelling creates tradition. The theme of memory and narrative are central to Metz's work.

In this setting, Metz sees formal doctrine as expressions of this subversive memory. In this regard, a key reference for Political Theology is a paper by Erik Peterson which looks at the political implications of the trinitarian formulations of the early Church. Peterson notes that monotheism carries with it a political program—one God, one empire, one emperor. (The same argument was used by Irenaeus to justify the concept of a monarchical bishop—one God, one Lord, one Church, one bishop!) Peterson argues that Christian belief in three persons in one God was, among other things, a rejection of this political program.

Finally, we might note Metz's definition of faith:

> The faith of Christians is a praxis in history and society that is to be understood as hope in solidarity in the God of Jesus as a God of the living and the dead who calls all men to be subjects in his presence. Christians justify themselves in this essentially apocalyptic praxis in their historical struggle for their fellow men. They stand up for all men in their attempt to become subjects in solidarity with each other. In this praxis they resist the danger of both a creeping evolutionary disintegration of the history of men as subjects and of an increasing negation of the individual in view of a new, post-middle-class image of man (p.73).

Here we see key themes to Metz's theology—apocalyptic, solidarity with the living and the dead, praxis, to be a subject.

Comments on theological method

While Metz describes his work as a contribution to a practical fundamental theology, there is clearly a difference in Metz's conception of fundamental theology and what Rahner has given us as his contribution to fundamental theology. Metz is seeking to analyze the fundamental human reality in a much fuller, more concrete manner than Rahner. His starting-point is not simply a philosophical anthropology, but also recognizes social and political dimensions to the person.

In terms of the functional specialties, Metz's work is, I think, again broader than Rahner's. Rahner works very much within the speciality of foundations, providing the foundation categories which anticipate future doctrines. Metz, on the other hand, works between the two areas of dialectics and foundations. Within the area of dialectics, Metz provides us with a hermeneutics of suspicion, analyzing the values and disvalues underlying various social forces, in particular asking for whose benefit these forces operate.

Out of a conversion experience which is mediated by the dangerous memory of the suffering of Jesus, Metz is then concerned not with providing philosophical categories which anticipate Christian doctrines, but with the new social realities which arise out of conversion, which find later expression in doctrine. These new social realities then act as a powerful prophetic critique of present social injustice. In this way, Metz's work illustrates the prophetic role of a foundational theology.

Metz's Political Theology has influenced and been influenced by Liberation Theology. It has had an impact on Feminist Theology. It has raised serious questions about the place of theology in Western society. As with Liberation Theology, its greatest problem is that of specifying alternative social structures which are credible and possible. However, it remains a significant cutting edge in contemporary theology.

DISCUSSION QUESTIONS

• How would you see the prophetic role of the theologian?

• Identify other dominant ideologies in our society. What effects do these have on our religious consciousness?

Bibliography

Rather than refer to further works of Metz, I will refer the reader to works which have been helpful to me in coming to grips with Metz's thought.
G. Baum, *Theology and Society*, New York: Paulist Press, 1987— a very readable collection of essays which touch on the questions raised in Political Theology.
R. Chopp, *The Praxis of Suffering*, Maryknoll, N.Y.: Orbis Books, 1986—an excellent study of political and liberation theologies, not as readable as Baum but more penetrating.
M. Lamb, *Solidarity with Victims*, New York: Crossroad, 1982— very solid and difficult work, but rewards perseverance.

For a "biblical" Political Theology there is the excellent work:

W. Brueggeman, *The Prophetic Imagination*, Philadelphia: Fortress Press, 1978.

CHAPTER 12

Jürgen Moltmann, *Dialectic Theology*

Since its founding with Martin Luther, Protestant theology has had a long tradition of dialectic theologizing, of contrasting God and humanity, sin and grace, the human condition with the glory to come. Protestant theology of the middle twentieth century was dominated by the dialectic theology of Karl Barth. The most significant contemporary exponent of such a theological style is undoubtedly Jürgen Moltmann.

Moltmann first came to prominence with his major work, *Theology of Hope* (1964), a book which brought together the eschatological influence of Barth's theology with the Marxist philosophy of the Jewish writer, Ernest Bloch. There Moltmann argues that eschatology is not simply another topic within theology but an issue which pervades the whole of our theological outlook (a stance not dissimilar to Pannenberg). This work was followed by *The Crucified God* (1972), a contemporary restatement of Luther's "theology of the cross," and *The Church in the Power of the Spirit* (1975), an ecclesiological and pneumatological study. This trilogy was preparatory to a major series on dogmatic theological concerns, the first of which to appear was *The Trinity and the Kingdom of God* (1980). Other works have since appeared on the doctrine of creation and Christology.

On the one hand, Moltmann's theology is classically Protestant, thoroughly biblical and grounded in a Lutheran perspective. There is not much concern here for a purely metaphysical theology. On the other hand, it is thoroughly contemporary, with a scholarly historical perspective and a deep concern for contemporary social and cultural issues. Perhaps no work illustrates this better than the one under consideration here, *The Trinity and the Kingdom of God*. While there are many fascinating aspects to this work, particularly Moltmann's discussion of the suffering of God, I have chosen to focus on the way in which he weaves theological and political issues together in his discussion of the Trinity as the model for a community free of dominion.

Work under consideration—*The Trinity and the Kingdom of God: The Doctrine of God*, New York/London: Harper & Row/SCM, 1981

This work represents Moltmann's major engagement with the Christian doctrine of the Trinity. Its main thesis is that the events of the death and resurrection of Jesus are not simply events in human history through which we gain our salvation. Rather they are a dramatic working out of events in the very life of the trinitarian God. For Moltmann the crucifixion and death of Jesus is the abandonment of the Son by the Father in which the Son suffers the loss of the Father and the Father suffers the loss of the Son. In this way the theological debate about the suffering of God (see, for example, the chapter on Dorothee Soelle) is given an explicitly trinitarian form. Human history then becomes the unfolding of the trinitarian life of God. This is a continuation of Moltmann's theology as developed in *The Crucified God* and is clearly influenced by the philosophy of Hegel.

In the development of this thesis, Moltmann not only seeks to ground it in the witness of the New Testament, he also engages in an ongoing dialogue with the whole theological tradition. Augustine and Aquinas are regularly mentioned, as are the more contemporary theologians, Karl Barth and Karl Rahner. The key threat which he sees as emerging within this tradition is the recurring problem of modalism. Modalism understands the Trinity in terms of the persons of the Trinity being three modes of being, or expression, of the one divine subject. According to this view the distinctions between Father, Son and Spirit are "for us"; they are not distinctions within the

Godhead. Moltmann is particularly critical of Barth and Rahner whom he sees as succumbing to the individualism of the age by positing in God one subject, one self-consciousness, one "I," who then expresses Godself in three different ways. Historically Moltmann traces this back to the Hegelian notion of God as the Absolute Subject (pp.139ff).

However, for Moltmann, the threat posed by modalism is not simply one of theological correctness or of heresy. It is also a problem for our understanding of how we organise our common life. The political equivalent of modalism is the rule of the absolute monarch. Modalism is one form of what he calls "monotheism" and "monotheism and monarchianism are only the names for two sides of the same thing: the One is the principle and point of integration for the Many" (p.130). Drawing on the work of Erik Peterson, he argues that there is a seductive power in monotheistic monarchianism which results in a religious-political ideology. The end result of such a strict monotheism is theocracy (a state where God is seen as the ultimate ruler), as exemplified in some Islamic states.

The Christian version of such a monotheism is found in the two heresies represented by Arius and Sabellius. Arius denied the reality of the Trinity by subordinating the Son to the Father. According to such belief there can be no essential unity between Father and Son; nor can Jesus lead us into a full fellowship with the Father. The rejection of Arius' position at the Council of Nicea (325 CE) was significant, according to Moltmann, not just theologically, but also politically. Because of God's trinitarian nature, "God's universal sovereignty can then no longer be understood as the 'universal monarch' to which everything is subjected" (p.134).

Sabellius' position, of the other hand, is strictly modalist. Whereas Arius sought to protect the divine unity by subordinating the Son to the Father, Sabellius sought to protect it by making the Father and Son (and the Spirit) modes of operation of the one divine subject. While liberal theology has been drawn to the Arian position, Moltmann argues that Western Church doctrine has continued to be infected with modalism. Indeed it is a "question which the Eastern church still puts to the whole trinitarian doctrine of the churches of the West" (p.136).

Moltmann takes up these ideas in more detail in the concluding chapter of his book where he seeks to develop a more positive account of the trinitarian "kingdom of freedom." Here he is developing an explicitly Political Theology, whose task he defines in terms of uncovering the "relationship between the religious ideas of any given era and the political constitution of its societies" (p.192). As opposed to an anti-trinitarian monotheism which grounds an autocratic, monarchical society, Moltmann argues that trinitarian faith grounds a true "kingdom of freedom."

Beginning with an account of what he calls "political monotheism," Moltmann identifies a relationship between philosophical monotheism and a "cosmological doctrine of the single hierarchical world order" (p.193). Indeed such a relationship can be found in the writings of Aristotle, who views the universe as ruled by one perfect, indivisible, immovable and impassible divine being. Applying this vision to human society, Aristotle declares, "Let there be only one ruler," since the rule of many is not healthy for the body politic.

Some Christian apologists were not slow to develop similar thinking in their relationship with the Roman empire. They argued that Christian belief in one God could help overcome the division caused by the many nations and their many gods throughout the Empire. Such a position became more acceptable as Christianity went from being a persecuted faith, to being tolerated, to eventually becoming the state religion. "The idea of unity in God therefore provokes both the idea of the universal, unified church, and the idea of the universal, unified state: one God—one emperor—one church—one empire" (p.195). Moltmann argues that this type of monotheism is one of the few elements of the Christian heritage to survive the European Enlightenment. There results a history of absolutism, both secular and religious, from the absolute monarchies of Europe to the theocracies of John Calvin. "If the divine sovereignty is made the prototype of the sovereignty of the state, what emerges is a hitherto unknown absolutism of power" (p.196).

A similar type of process can be seen within the Church as well. Here Moltmann refers to clerical monotheism, and he identifies its prototypical exponent in the writings of Ignatius of Antioch. Ignatius:

... founded the episcopal unity of the church by means of the following theological hierarchy: one God—one Christ—one bishop—one church. The bishop represents Christ to his church just as Christ represents God. This representative derivation of divine authority is obviously monarchical monotheism. The church's hierarchy is supposed to correspond to and represent the divine monarchy (p.200).

In particular Moltmann is very critical of the extension of such an ideology to the papal office. Indeed he finds the theological justification of the papal office to be dominated by monotheistic thinking. As in the case of political absolutism, monarchical monotheism is used as an ideological buttress to support the hierarchical nature of the church.

If political and clerical absolutism is the result of a monarchical monotheism, what would be the consequences of taking a truly trinitarian vision of God as the basis for a political theology? Here Moltmann offers a number of suggestions.

The trinitarian God provides no model for the omnipotent, universal monarch. The unity of Father, Son and Spirit is not the unity of a single ruler. Nor is God the archetype of worldly "mighty ones." Rather God is the Father of Jesus, crucified and raised. In this way God reveals not power, but love, passionate and suffering love. The glory of God is revealed not in crowns and victories but in the community of Christ, the fellowship of believers and the poor. Rather than being a group of people defined in terms of privileges and subjugation, in a trinitarian community people "are defined through their relations with one another and in their significance for one another, not in opposition to one another" (p.198). A trinitarian community is one which is with one another, for one another and in one another, just as the life of the persons of the Trinity is a common life.

In this way a trinitarian doctrine harmonizes personality and sociality, personalism and socialism. "A Christian doctrine of the Trinity compels us to develop a social personalism and a personal socialism" (p.199). Such a stance overcomes the individualism of the present era, which Moltmann traces back in part to Augustine's psychological analogy for the Trinity, based on the conscious operations of a single individual.

To counter these monarchical distortions of our secular and ecclesial societies Moltmann develops a trinitarian doctrine of freedom and the Kingdom. Inspired by the thought of Joachim of Fiore (a twelfth-century Italian monk who saw history as divided into three ages, one each for the Father, Son and Spirit), he speaks of the Kingdom of the Father, Son and Spirit in distinctive ways. The Kingdom of the Father is a world open to the future. The reign of the Father is not that of an almighty despot who destroys our freedom, but rather a place where our finite freedom is given space to move and time to grow. The Kingdom of the Son is the Lordship of the crucified savior and the fellowship of his brothers and sisters. Through his vicarious suffering we are freed from our servitude to sin. The Kingdom of the Spirit is experienced in the divine energies conferred as a gift on those liberated by the Son. Through this gift we lay hold of the freedom won for us by the Son. Finally there is the Kingdom of glory, yet to come, which is the consummation of the Father's creation, the universal establishment of the liberation gained by the Son, and the fulfillment of our divinization by the Spirit.

This trinitarian vision of the Kingdom of God then translates into Moltmann's trinitarian doctrine of human freedom. Here he contrasts an individualistic, liberal view of freedom with a view of freedom grounded in interdependence. The former pits the freedom of one against the freedom of the other. Each is free except where it infringes on the freedom of another person. To increase my freedom will involve a struggle for power and possession over and against the other. Such freedom can only be at the cost of another. The latter understands freedom in interpersonal terms, where my freedom is grounded in the love and respect of others and my love and respect for them. The other is then not a competitor in the realm of freedom, but a mutual participant. The other does not limit my freedom but expands it. "That is the social side of freedom. We call it love and solidarity" (p.216). This is the freedom to which God calls us. Indeed, "only the passionate God, the God who suffers by virtue of his passion for people, calls the freedom of men and women to life" (p.218). We can see here Moltmann's interest in the question of divine suffering.

Moltmann then brings together these reflections on freedom

with his trinitarian vision of the Kingdom, to present three "strata in the concept of freedom." In the Kingdom of the Father freedom is that of the servants of God. However, the experience of being a servant of God is not one of oppression. It is a title not of humiliation, but of honor. To be used and needed by God gives our lives meaning, raising us above the rest of creation. In the Kingdom of the Son, the inward quality of this freedom is changed, as we become children of the Father, through fellowship with the Son. Moltmann insists that this is only becomes possible "where the Son appears," that is, as a consequence of the Incarnation. Children, of course, cannot be dismissed like servants. Their place in the household is assured. They are heirs, and their freedom is found in their intimate relationship with the Father. In the Kingdom of the Spirit, there is again a change in the inward quality of freedom. Not only are we called to be servants and children, but also friends of God. We thus enter into a new and "direct" relationship with God, where we know ourselves in God and God in us. In this account he differs from Joachim of Fiore, who understood the Kingdoms of Father, Son and Spirit to refer to three distinct historical epochs.

What we can witness in Moltmann's theology is a powerful combination of theological and political themes. In his hands the doctrine of the Trinity is transformed so as to reveal a socio-political relevance unrecognised by previous generations. Now the doctrine of the Trinity can be seen as promoting a "social personalism and a personal socialism," overcoming the rampant individualism of the West and the deadening State collectivism of the Communist bloc. This is far and away from the Enlightenment position of Emmanuel Kant who could discern no possible practical consequences of the doctrine of the Trinity. For Moltmann the doctrine of the Trinity is eminently practical in its consequences for our political life.

Comments on theological method

The dialectical heritage of Moltmann's theology is evident in the breadth and power of his sweeping rhetoric. One is imme-diately struck by the impact of Moltmann's rejection of what he calls "monotheism," by which he means, a non-trinitarian monotheism. Most Christians would almost automatically think of themselves as "monotheist," though it is perhaps fair to say that most, too, would find it difficult to explain how their trinitarian faith differs from tritheism. Moltmann's stance certainly startles us into reassessing the nature of our Christian beliefs, by establishing a dialectical opposition between what we felt comfortable with, that is, monotheism, and what we profess to believe, that is, the Trinity. However, once such an opposition is established, it does become difficult to see how Moltmann can avoid the charge of tritheism. Indeed a number of critics have suggested that his position is tritheistic, despite his denials.

Criticisms have also been made of Moltmann's way of handling the question of divine suffering. Dorothee Soëlle, who herself speaks of divine suffering, fears that, in Moltmann's hands, the theme of divine suffering becomes a justification for suffering, rather than a protest against it. Leonardo Boff has similarly complained of a "profound lack of theological rigor" in Moltmann's discussion of this topic.

Perhaps we can shed some light on these criticisms by a consideration of Moltmann's theological method. The above material focuses on the question of trinitarian doctrine. In that sense it belongs to the functional specialty of doctrines, moving into the area of systematics, as he seeks to understand the political consequences of the doctrine. In Lonergan's schema these processes should occur after the specialty of foundations. And it is here that we may be able to locate the cause of the concerns expressed by Moltmann's critics.

According to Lonergan the task of foundations is to provide the required control of meaning and the necessary categories, which are expressive of our basic Christian commitments. Both these provide questions which can be addressed to Moltmann's work. Take, for example, Moltmann's distinction between the Kingdoms of the Father, Son and Spirit. While Moltmann makes a conceptual distinction between these, one is entitled to ask whether this is a real distinction or not. Are we simply multiplying concepts without any underlying control of the meaning of our terms? Similarly, from where do these categories arise? Certainly not from the Scriptures, which speak only of the Kingdom of God. What then grounds them? Are they the correct categories to use, or do they just sound good? Of course this is not to say that Moltmann could not address such questions in his own way. But to do so would require something more than he has presented in the present work. Perhaps this is the concern over "theological rigor" which Boff has identified with respect to Moltmann's work.

Moltmann himself has drawn attention to the provisional nature of his theological project. He does not see his work as providing a definitive dogmatic or systematic theology, since on his understanding such an achievement is simply not possible. In that sense, it is likely that he could acknowledge some loose ends and unanswered questions in his work. Any theologian will always trade off the desire to say something against the inability to say everything. Each is forced to make his or her own compromises. And it is clear that all can acknowledge the contribution that Moltmann has made to our understanding of the Trinity, especially in terms of its political consequences. He has made it abundantly clear that Christian faith does not exist in some purely "spiritual realm" unconcerned with and disconnected from very real, concrete sociopolitical concerns. It is his insistence on exploring the political consequences of Christian faith which have marked him as a leading theologian of the present era.

DISCUSSION QUESTIONS

- Moltmann has drawn out some of the political consequences of the doctrine of the Trinity. Can you think of others? Can you identify other Christian doctrines which may similarly have political consequences? You might consider, for example, the doctrines of creation and original sin.

- How do you respond to Moltmann's criticisms of "monotheism"? Would you understand Christianity as monotheistic? Do you think he has been sufficiently careful to avoid the problem of tritheism?

Bibliography

Moltmann has been particularly prolific over the years. The following works are just some of his output.

Theology of Hope, New York: Harper and Row, 1967—this early work brought Moltmann to the attention of the theological world. It was highly influential in the development of Liberation Theology.

The Crucified God, New York/London: Harper & Row/SCM, 1974—his early exploration of the relationship between the crucifixion of Jesus and trinitarian theology; in that sense a precursor to *The Trinity and the Kingdom of God*.

The Church in the Power of the Spirit, New York/London: Harper & Row/SCM, 1977—not to neglect the Holy Spirit, this work considers the work of the Spirit in relationship to the nature of the Church.

The Way of Jesus Christ, London: SCM, 1990—a radical Christology of discipleship.

History and the Triune God, New York/London: Crossroad/ SCM, 1991—extends the exploration of *The Trinity and the Kingdom of God*. For Moltmann not only is the Trinity active in history, but the Trinity itself has a history, through the death and resurrection of Jesus.

God—His and Hers, New York/London: Crossroad/SCM, 1991—written with his wife and fellow-theologian, Elisabeth Moltmann-Wendel, this book explores the place of gender in determining our images of and relationship to God.

His most recent work is:

The Coming of God, London: SCM, 1996—a study of Christian eschatology.

CHAPTER 13

Gustavo Gutiérrez, *Liberation Theology I*

Gustavo Gutiérrez is one of the founding fathers of Liberation Theology. His main work, *A Theology of Liberation*, is the standard basic reference in the area, though it was one of the first books to be written which dealt specifically with Liberation Theology. Its significance is indicated by the fact that it has recently been republished in a fifteenth anniversary edition. Liberation Theology itself is one of the bright new stars on the theological horizon. Its geographic origin is the turbulent continent of South America, which has had a long history of social and political upheaval. Liberation Theology is an attempt to make a particularly theological contribution to and analysis of those upheavals.

Since its inception it has been surrounded by controversy. Its commitment to the poor and oppressed and its use of Marxist categories and means of analysis has come up against right-wing military dictatorships, and Church authorities who have been anxious to preserve the historically close relations between Church and State which have existed in South America. Even the Vatican has been drawn into the debate. The Sacred Congregation for the Doctrine of the Faith has issued two "instructions" on the theme of liberation, one pointing out the dangers of the use of Marxist categories, the other noting the positive gains that Liberation Theology represents.

Liberation Theology is one of the first major attempts to do a local theology, i.e. one which draws on the concrete experience and situation of a local people. Its focus is on the particular situation in South America, with its huge disparity between rich and poor, with its various military governments and its history of uneven economic development. Yet its particular focus raises questions about the very nature of Christianity and of theology, particularly in relation to the modern world. It is because of this that Liberation Theology has implications which extend beyond the boundaries of South America to the whole Church. It is not necessarily the answers which Liberation Theology gives which are important, so much as the questions it asks. Such questions, once raised, will not go away, a lesson we should have learnt from the Modernist crisis.

Material under consideration—*A Theology of Liberation*,[1] Maryknoll, N.Y.: Orbis Books, 1973, revised edition, 1988

Gutiérrez begins his book with a discussion on the nature of theology. He considers two traditional understandings of theology, theology as wisdom and theology as rational knowledge, and compares them with an understanding which is prevalent in Liberation Theology. Liberation Theology defines theology as critical reflection on praxis. Praxis is a central concept of Liberation Theology. It refers to committed action in the social, political sphere. Gutiérrez traces the Christian understanding of praxis from a central focus on charity, through Ignatian spirituality, to recent talk about reading the signs of the times. Praxis is also central to Marxist philosophy, indeed, to many modern philosophies. Gutiérrez notes with approval Marx's comment that the point of philosophy is not to interpret the world but to change it! (On this criterion Marx was very successful!)

One should note also that theology is defined as a critical reflection on praxis. It is critical not just in the epistemological sense of Kant, but also critical with regard to the economic and sociocultural aspects of life. It critically analyzes the economic and cultural presuppositions which a theologian brings to his or her work, seeking out hidden ideological assumptions. Such a theology is not naive about its own political implications:

Theology as critical reflection thus fulfills a liberating function for humankind and the Christian community, preserving them from fetishism and idolatry, as well as from a pernicious and belittling narcissism (p.10).

In particular, such a theology takes a stance, one which identifies with the poor and suffering. It involves a "preferential option for the poor" or a solidarity with and for the poor. (The phrase "preferential option for the poor," which has become the hallmark of Liberation Theology, does not, as far as I know, appear in this work. Gutiérrez does, however, speak of solidarity with the poor.)

One of the difficulties with this conception is that it inverts what is seen as the traditional priority of orthodoxy, right teaching, and "orthopraxis," right action. A traditional view saw orthopraxis as flowing out of orthodoxy—people did the right thing if they believed the right things. It took its stand on the axiom, nothing can be loved unless it is known. Such a position places great emphasis on having the right doctrines, with faith as an intellectual assent to correct propositions.

Liberation Theology, on the other hand, places the emphasis on action, on committing oneself to the task of transforming the world in the light of the Gospel. It is in the experience of this struggle that one comes to a correct knowledge of God, to orthodoxy. Theology is, then, reflection on pastoral practice; it begins "at sundown." Such reflection, of course, will help inform future pastoral activity, but the priority remains with praxis rather than "doxy."

The pastoral activity of the Church does not flow as a conclusion from theological premises. Theology does not produce pastoral activity; rather it reflects upon it. Theology must be able to find in pastoral activity the presence of the Spirit inspiring the action of the Christian community (p.9).

What Liberation Theology (through Gutiérrez) is giving us here is a new theological paradigm, a new way of doing theology:

The theology of liberation attempts to reflect on the experience and meaning of the faith based on the commitment to abolish injustice and to build a new society; this theology must be verified by the practice of that commitment, by active, effective participation in the struggle which the exploited classes have undertaken against their oppressors (p.307).

It is not difficult to see in this quote the influence of the Marxist concept of class struggle. The role and place of this concept in Liberation Theology will be discussed later.

Central to this stage of Liberation Theology's project is its analysis of the situation in Latin America. It is described as being at the periphery, on the outer, of the modern capitalist world, where the first world is the center. Latin America is seen as dependent economically, socially and culturally, and this dependence is integral to the process of development that occurs in the first world. On this analysis, the first world is dependent on the third for its own wealth and development— development and underdevelopment go hand in hand! Gutiérrez sees this as an international form of the class struggle, with poor nations struggling to free themselves from the domination of the rich.

This analysis is the so-called dependency theory, which was a common sociological analysis in the 1960s. Several critics of Liberation Theology have noted its use of this dependency theory. It is a theory which has since been criticized within sociology. In the introduction to the revised edition, Gutiérrez admits the inadequacy of dependency theory to analyze what is really a very complex question of development and underdevelopment (p.xxiv). However, such are the risks one must take if one is to use current theories from the social sciences to help clarify social situations. The alternative is to say nothing!

Based on the Latin American experience, Gutiérrez claims that the path out of this situation is not one of developmentalism, the gradual process of economic development into a modern capitalist state. This has been tried and has failed, often leading to greater suffering for the poor. Instead, Gutiérrez claims, what is needed is liberation, a revolutionary new social and economic system.

This theme of liberation is not the creation *ex nihilo* of Liberation Theology. Liberation Theology takes its stand on new readings of scripture which are more sensitive to the historical circumstances of the scriptural authors. The theme of human liberation can be found in the Bible, especially in the Book of Exodus and in denunciations made by the prophets of the social injustices within Israel. The theme of human liberation has also found its place in the social encyclicals of the Church, especially *Populorum Progressio* and the more recent social encyclicals of John Paul II.

Of particular importance to Liberation Theology have been the statements issued by the bishops of Latin America in the conferences at Medellin and Puebla. (Puebla occurred after the publication of *A Theology of Liberation*, but remains influential for later developments.) These statements and the activities within the Church which flowed from them have created a new presence of the Church in Latin America.

Gutiérrez sees five main themes emerging from these (see pp.68–71). Firstly, the Church has a role of prophetic denunciation of the injustices within Latin American society. The task of denunciation is a duty for the Church, which arises out of its solidarity with the poor. Further, through such denunciation the Church signals its intention to disassociate itself from the unjust social order with which it has long been identified. This task is both critical and constructive, critical of existing structures of domination, but constructive in encouraging humanizing elements within society.

Secondly, there is a need for a conscientizing evangelization, i.e. one which educates, inspires, stimulates and helps orient all of the initiatives that contribute to the formation of the human person. Such an evangelization will help identify and hand on the "revolutionary thrust" of the doctrinal riches of the Gospel. It will work to break down the idea of an other-worldly salvation cut off from the concerns of social liberation.

Thirdly, it is the Church's task to be in solidarity with the poor and oppressed people of Latin America. Such a solidarity cannot be merely rhetorical but must be a real solidarity. It involves not only evangelization of the poor and denunciation of injustice, but also simplicity of lifestyle. It is a call to evangelical poverty, which gives expression to a solidarity with the poor.

Fourthly, given the demands of these three, the Church needs to look to itself, to reform its own structures where these have become a block to the preaching of the Gospel. The experiences of prophetic denunciation, conscientizing evangelization, and solidarity with the poor have led people to recognize the inadequacy of Church structures and pastoral strategy. One response to this has been the development of base Church communities (see the next chapter on Boff's book, *Ecclesiogenesis*). Finally, Gutiérrez sees a need for a change in lifestyle among the clergy, towards adopting a lifestyle which reflects a commitment to the creation of a new society.

The main theological question which Liberation Theology raises is the relationship between liberation, as a social, economic reality, and salvation as a "religious" reality. This is the central problem in Liberation Theology. Gutiérrez strongly argues that salvation cannot be limited to a sphere of life labelled "religious." Neither is it an individualistic notion. Inasmuch as salvation reaches out into the social and economic spheres of human existence, it will be experienced as a liberation from oppression. Thus "we can say that the historical, political liberation event is the growth of the Kingdom and is a salvific event; but it is not the coming of the Kingdom, not all of salvation" (p.104).

It is in the area of the connection between social liberation and "religious" salvation that Liberation Theology has caused most debate. Many would claim that, by establishing such a link, Liberation Theology undermines traditional eschatology, reducing heaven to a social utopia. Liberation Theology is very aware of the Marxist critique of religion, and especially a futurist eschatology which would placate people in the present with promises of heaven in a future life. However, it is also aware of the dangers in identifying any particular political movement with the coming of the kingdom. Every such attempt must be judged by the "eschatological proviso," that the kingdom is always "not yet." What we are faced with is a steadfast refusal on the part of Liberation Theology to divorce religion/faith from the real social, political and economic conditions of people's lives.

However, it is clear that the concept of utopia has played a significant role in the thought of Liberation Theology. For Gutiérrez, it refers to a "historical plan for a qualitatively different society." It expresses an "aspiration to establish new social relations among human beings" (p.135). The concept of utopia acts as a denunciation of the existing order as well as an annunciation of a new vision, a new social order. As such, it helps with the emergence of a new social consciousness. Further, Gutiérrez distinguishes utopia from ideology, which he sees as always in danger of dogmatizing some existing political or social movement. Utopia keeps alive the "eschatological proviso." On the other hand, critics of Liberation Theology, such as Michael Novak, have found it to be very vague as to what it concretely proposes for a new social order, too utopian and not specific enough in its analysis.

In all this, we see that history is a key theme for Liberation Theology. Not history as an abstract concept—the person as historical—but the concrete history of suffering and oppression that is the reality in Latin America. The question is, how does faith relate to this situation? What is at stake is not just the meaning of theology, but "the very meaning of Christianity" (p.49). "What does it mean to be a Christian" in a world of suffering and oppression? This is the urgent question that Liberation Theology addresses to the Christian tradition.

Comments on theological method

Central to the project which Liberation Theology has undertaken is its creative dialogue with and dependence on the social sciences. Liberation Theology theologizes about the social reality. It does not claim to have direct access to this reality, but seeks the help of the social sciences to clarify and systematize the social order. Within the social sciences there are two basic approaches, the functionalist, based on a metaphor of organic unities and hierarchies, and the conflictual, which sees society in terms of a struggle between competing groups. Liberation Theology opts for the latter as a more accurate reflection of the situation in Latin America. The adoption of such a conflictual model can also be found in the social teaching of John Paul II.

However, the most common form of conflictual model in the social sciences is that of Marxism. For this reason, Liberation Theology has been criticized for its use of Marxist concepts, particularly class struggle. The document from the Sacred Congregation for the Doctrine of the Faith, *Instruction on Certain Aspects of Liberation Theology*, argues that once one makes use of any Marxist concepts, one is necessarily led to adopting all of Marxism, which is materialistic, atheistic and deterministic. However, this seems a doubtful proposition. On the other hand, it is fair to note that Gutiérrez does tend to treat Marxism as "scientific," without any critical recognition of the difficulties associated with such a claim. However, later liberation theologies have become much more sophisticated in their use of the social sciences.

It is important to note also that Liberation Theology addresses a different social context to the dominant social contexts addressed by European and North American theologies. The social context of European theology, in particular, is that of a post-Enlightenment secular society, in which religion has become marginalized and hence seeks to defend its own relevance. The Latin American social context has been one of massive poverty and social oppression. Its concern is not the justification of religion but the prophetic call for justice.

In terms of the functional specialties discussed in Chapter 4, we can see that the work of Gutiérrez can perhaps best be understood in terms of conversion, foundations and doctrines.

What calls us to conversion is the plight of the poor. It is this focus on the poor which is central to all Liberation Theology. Their situation calls for a change of heart, a commitment, a reordering of priorities:

> I have already pointed out the important role played in Christian consciousness by the irruption of the poor into our history. . . . (T)his new presence has made us aware that our partners in dialogue are the poor, those who are "non-persons"—that is, those who are not considered to be human beings with full rights (p.xxix).

This conversion experience is given expression and formulated within a foundational framework. Here, we find Gutiérrez drawing on both the biblical prophetic tradition and contemporary social sciences to provide the basic categories of justice, salvation, liberation and class conflict, through which the conversion can be made explicit.

Finally, we arrive at a new theological "doctrine," one which may be called the "preferential option for the poor."[2] This theological doctrine, which has been taken up in various forms in the encyclicals and addresses of John Paul II, is a major contribution of Liberation Theology to the Church's self-understanding.

DISCUSSION QUESTIONS

• If the "preferential option for the poor" were to be officially defined as part of Christian faith, what implications would it have for Christian living?

• What would you see as the advantages/disadvantages for theology of the use of Marxist categories?

Bibliography

Gutiérrez's book was one of the first available in English which treated the topic of Liberation Theology. Since then, there have been countless books written. Though Gutiérrez is often considered one of the founding fathers of Liberation Theology, he has not been as prolific a writer as others, such as Juan Luis Segundo or Leonardo Boff. Gutiérrez's other works include:
On Job: God-Talk and the Suffering of the Innocent, Maryknoll, N.Y.: Orbis Books, 1987—a detailed study of the Book of Job. Gutiérrez looks at the plight of Job in the light of the innocent suffering of so many in South America.
The Power of the Poor in History, Maryknoll, N.Y.: Orbis Books, 1983.
We Drink from Our Own Wells, Maryknoll, N.Y.: Orbis Books, 1984—a work on the spirituality of Liberation Theology.
Las Casas: In Search of the Poor of Jesus Christ, Maryknoll, N.Y.: Orbis Books, 1992—this is a major study of Bartolomé de Las Casas (1474–1566), an early Dominican missionary to Latin America. He argued for the full humanity of the conquered

peoples, thus beginning a tradition of Liberation Theology.

An analysis of Gutiérrez's work can be found in:

R. Chopp, *The Praxis of Suffering*, Maryknoll, N.Y.: Orbis Books, 1986.

On the questions raised by the use of Marxist social analysis in Liberation Theology consider:

A.F. McGovern, *Marxism: An American Christian Perspective*, Maryknoll, N.Y.: Orbis Books, 1980.

On the place of the "option for the poor" in Church teaching:

D. Dorr, *Option for the Poor: A Hundred Years of Vatican Social Teaching*, Maryknoll, N.Y./Dublin: Orbis Books/Gill and Macmillan, 1983.

For a synthesis of Liberation Theology:

R. Haight, *An Alternative Vision: An Interpretation of Liberation Theology*, New York: Paulist Press, 1985.

For a critique of Liberation Theology from a capitalist perspective:

M. Novak, *Will It Liberate?*, New York: Paulist Press, 1986.

Further works will be cited at the end of the chapter on Leonardo Boff.

---

1. Throughout I shall refer to the revised edition. In particular, I have drawn on material in the Introduction to that edition.

2. However inadequately; see Gutiérrez's own reservations about the terminology in his Introduction to the revised edition, p.xxvi.

CHAPTER 14

Leonardo Boff, *Liberation Theology II*

Another key figure in Liberation Theology is Leonardo Boff, who has written several books in the area. Boff is a prolific writer, whose key works include *Jesus Christ Liberator, Ecclesiogenesis*, and *Church, Charism and Power*. Boff came to international attention when he received an official rebuff from the Sacred Congregation for the Doctrine of the Faith. His suspension from teaching for a year was described as a "sabbatical" to give him time to revise his opinions. However, after a concerted stand by the Brazilian bishops, his suspension was lifted after eleven months and he has resumed his normal activities. The cause of complaint was Boff's writing on the Church, in *Church, Charism and Power*, in which he was highly critical of the way authority has been exercised within the Church. His conflicts with Roman authorities continued, however, and in recent years Boff has left the priesthood though he continues to work as a theologian.

Something of the context in which Boff writes can be seen in the preface of his book, *Jesus Christ Liberator*. Here he states that at the time the book was being written, the word *liberation* " ... was forbidden to be used in all the communications media" (p.xii). This gives a good indication of how, in such a situation, theology can become a political act. Within the Brazilian context, there has always been a close connection between the Church and the political scene. Traditionally, the Church was seen to stand with the status quo in return for certain privileges granted by the state. More recently, certain sections of the Church have taken their stand with the poor and marginalized within the society. The Church's work to help liberate the poor from their poverty was bound to create opposition from the rich and powerful. Liberation Theology grew out of this struggle to identify with the poor.

Central to the pastoral strategy of the Brazilian Church has been the development of base Church communities. Boff has himself been deeply involved in working with such communities. It is his involvement with these communities that has led Boff to develop his ideas in the area of ecclesiology (theology of the Church). In the Franciscan tradition, to which he belongs, Boff has a vision of a Church founded amongst the poor, a Church which renounces its allegiances with the rich and powerful, and which lives out the radical, evangelical call of the Gospel. Such a vision was bound to disturb those who are called to maintain the visible structures of the Church.

This work among the poor, a pastoral expression of the preferential option for the poor, illustrates well the "political" nature of Liberation Theology. Its critics have accused Liberation Theology of "politicizing" the Church. Yet, as the history of the Latin American Church makes clear, the Church has always been "politicized." Liberation Theology is not a "politicization" but a shift in the political stance of the Church. As a significant social body, the Church cannot help but have a political influence. The question is on whose behalf does the Church exercise this influence, her own or that of the poor and marginalized?

Material under consideration—*Ecclesiogenesis*, Maryknoll/London: Orbis/Collins, 1986

In his book, *Ecclesiogenesis*, Boff writes of the experience of the new base Church communities in "reinventing" the Church. Even the use of such a term as "reinventing" is bound to raise difficulties. Is this a new Church different from the one true Church? Why does the Church require "reinventing" since it already exists? To many the term would sound schismatic. Yet this is clearly not Boff's intention. His objective is to draw attention to the fact that something new is happening in the Church with the experience of base Church communities. To this end, new experiences will lead to new questions and perhaps new answers to old questions. Hence, Boff concludes his book with a consideration of three *quaestiones disputatae* (disputed questions): Did the historical Jesus will only one institutional form for the Church? Is lay celebration of the Eucharist possible? Is women's priesthood possible?

Significantly, Boff begins his discussion of the Church with a sociological analysis of the distinction between society and community. I say "significantly" because one of the distinctive features of Liberation Theology is its willingness to draw upon insights from the social sciences and apply them to their theology. This is a significant change in methodology from traditional theology, which derived most of its categories from philosophy.

Boff notes that sociology has gone beyond a position which contrasts community and society, as found in the seminal sociological studies of Ferdinand Toennies. Such a position speaks of community in terms of "reciprocity" and "belonging," and society in terms of "anonymity" and "alienation." Boff draws on the work of the Latin American sociologist, Pedro Demo, and his study of the "sociological problems of community." For Demo, concrete human living always experiences a tension between communitarian and societal characteristics. A classless society, a society free from any structures of inequality and stratified roles, free from any conflict, is unrealistic. Institutionalization is inevitable in any group that wants to last longer than a generation. Such a move, however, will always threaten the communitarian spirit, which is thus in need of constant revitalization.

Applying this to the Church, Boff recognizes the role to be played by both institutionalized elements (e.g. hierarchy) and communitarian elements (base Church communities):

> These poles abide forever. The real problem resides in the manner in which both are lived, the one as well as the other: whether one pole seeks to absorb the other, cripple it, liquidate it, or each respects the other and opens itself to the other in constant willingness to be put to the question (p.7).

Still Boff recognizes a priority between the two. The institutional exists for the sake of the community, not vice versa— "the [community] must ever preserve its primacy. The [institutional] lives in function of the [community]" (p.7).

This sociological analysis raises the theological question of the relationship between particular Church and global Church, between Church as it exists within a local community and the Church as a global, universal institution. Before taking up this question, Boff must first establish that the base Church communities can properly be called Church. He notes that there are differing theological opinions as to whether such communities can properly be called Churches. Boff argues that, since they have the same goals as the universal Church, "to lead all men and women to the full communion of life with the Father and one another, through Jesus Christ, in the gift of the Holy Spirit, by means of the mediating activity of the church" (p.12), then they do indeed constitute a true and authentic presence of the Catholic Church.

What is significant in this analysis is the newness of the situation being analyzed:

> If we are to develop a new ecclesiology, we shall need more than just theological perspicacity and historico-dogmatic erudition. **We must face the new experience of church in our midst.** We ... are confronted with a new concretization of church without the presence of consecrated ministers and without the eucharistic celebration. It is not that this absence is not felt, is not painful. It is rather that these ministers do not exist in sufficient numbers. **This historical situation does not cause the church to disappear** (p.13) (emphasis added).

It is the newness of the situation which causes Boff to raise his *quaestiones disputatae* at the end of his book. New experiences may lead to new insights out of which may develop a new ecclesiology. Old answers may need to be revised, or at least tested in the light of these experiences.

Boff's preferred way of speaking of this new event is to speak of the "reinvention" of the Church. While acknowledging the complementary roles of community and institution, he argues for the priority of community. Where the community comes into being in the life of base Church communities, the Church is truly being "reinvented." Still, Boff does not see this as a human work, but the work of the Holy Spirit, the "true source of the ongoing birth and creation of the Church" (p.23). In this process of "reinvention," the first moment is a community of basic equality without distinctions of sex, nation or intelligence. In the second moment, however, differences arise, hierarchy develops, within the basic and primary unity. Such differences arise for the sake of the life of the community.

With such an understanding of Church, it make no sense, to Boff, to think of Jesus as making the Twelve some type of prototype hierarchy of a future Church. Hierarchy exists only for the sake of the community which it serves. Hence, Boff claims "Jesus established the Twelve as a community: as a messianic, eschatological church" (p.28). This basic community then spread out to form new apostolic communities. Within these communities there are a variety of ministries, one of which is to provide unity and order to the whole. The ministry of presiding over the community, be it "monitor" in a base Church community, priest in a parish, bishop in the diocese, or pope over the whole Church, is one of being a principle of unity within the local community and with the Church as a whole. Thus:

> [T]here is no such thing as absolute ordination. There is no such thing as a monitor without a community, a pastor without a parish, a bishop without a diocese. The Councils of Nicea (325) and Chalcedon (451) therefore considered absolute ordinations null (p.28).

Such a vision of Church obviously gives much greater prominence to the role of the laity, whose formation of community is the first moment in the life of the Church.

Boff concludes this first section of his book with material drawn from the actual experiences of base Church communities. While this is of immense value in understanding the ferment from which Boff's Liberation Theology springs, I prefer to spend the remaining space in consideration of the first of Boff's *quaestiones disputatae*—"Did the historical Jesus will only one institutional form for the Church?"

This question is not one of idle intellectual curiosity. If the historical Jesus did will only one institutional form and his so doing is normative for the Church, then the modes of institutional expression open to the base Church communities are necessarily limited. If the hierarchical structure of ordained priest and laity is part of that structure, then the base Church communities cannot even bear the name Church, since many are without the services of an ordained priest and depend for their coordination on a lay community "monitor." On the other hand, as we have already seen, Boff has argued that the base Christian communities are indeed properly "Church." Hence his interest in this disputed question. It is his stand for the base Christian communities which will shape his answer to it.

When Boff gives his theological analysis, however, the question of the base Christian communities does not play a direct role but simply forms part of the background scenery. His strictly theological argumentation is basically standard, drawing on the ecclesiological studies of Küng, Schnackenberg, Ratzinger and others. While Liberation Theology is a reflection on praxis, it does not hesitate to draw on standard theological sources. Moreover, Boff does not see his theological opinion as the only legitimate one, or even the only respectable one. However, he does see his opinion as one which could give a theological grounding for the base Church communities.

Following the lead of many New Testament scholars and modern ecclesiologists, Boff sees Jesus' ministry as one not of founding a Church but of preaching the Kingdom in the context of the conversion of Israel. It is only in the light of Jesus' failure to convert Israel that the Church comes into being. Thus, the Church is not part of the intention of the historical Jesus, but arises from a commission of the Risen Jesus. The passage Matthew 16:18–19, where Jesus commissions Peter as the rock on which he will build his Church, is seen as a post-resurrection account which Matthew places within the body of his Gospel.

In his understanding of the Church as a post-resurrectional reality, Boff draws on the work of Erik Peterson, whose ideas were also picked up and carried further by Joseph Ratzinger. Boff presents and briefly defends the following theses of Peterson:

1) The church exists only contingently upon the fact that the Jews, God's chosen people, did not believe in the Lord. It is of the very concept of the church that it is a church of Gentiles.
2) The Church exists only contingently upon the fact that the second coming of Jesus was not imminent: in other words, that concrete eschatology was suspended and in its place the doctrine of the last end of the human being had entered the picture.
3) The church exists only contingently upon the fact that the twelve apostles, called and inspired by the Holy Spirit, determined to go to the Gentiles (pp.56–57).

If such is the case, then Boff argues that it does not make sense to speak of Jesus historically willing only one institutional form for the Church. Rather,

Jesus willed, and continues to will, that form for his church which the apostolic community, enlightened by the Holy Spirit and confronted with the urgencies of its concrete situation, decided and in all responsibility assumed (p.60).

Clearly, Boff sees the base Church communities as a new concrete situation, which confronts the Church with new urgencies and so calls for new institutional forms which the Church may in all responsibility assume. These new institutional forms may include provision for the commissioning of lay community monitors by their communities to preside at eucharistic celebrations in the absence of a priest (Boff's second disputed question) and the ordination of women (Boff's third disputed question). The second disputed question is one also considered in the book *Ministry* by Edward Schillebeeckx. The third is one frequently raised in Feminist Theology, but also by many other theologians who can see no reason for barring women from ordained ministry.

In the beginning of our presentation of Boff's work, we noted his use of sociological categories to analyze the relationship between communitarian and hierarchical elements within the Church. Much of his subsequent argument depends on his understanding of the priority of communitarian over hierarchical elements. Some may object to the use of sociology to analyze a divine reality such as the Church. However, for a Church which has often understood itself as a complete (perfect) society, and which has understood the action of the divine as completing and perfecting nature but not destroying or undermining it, such an analysis is not only allowable but necessary, if we are to develop a theology of Church. Whatever the strengths and weaknesses of Boff's analysis, his use of sociological categories marks a significant addition to ecclesiology.

Comments on theological method

It is not easy to uncover or categorize the theological method that Boff is using. In this work, *Ecclesiogenesis*, Boff has not given us a fully-developed ecclesiology. As the printing notes indicate, two chapters had an independent existence but were then incorporated into this larger work. This does not contribute to the overall unity of the book. On the other hand, Boff himself would characterize his book as a systematic reflection on the actual praxis of the base Church communities. This is consistent with Liberation Theology's self-understanding and the priority it gives to praxis.

While respecting the right of Liberation Theology to specify its own theological method, part of the aim of this book is to consider the methodologies of various theologians within a unified framework. Thus, without wishing to do violence to Boff's approach, I would offer the following analysis.

In terms of the functional specialties mentioned in Chapter 4, it seems to me that Boff's work falls mainly within the first four, research, interpretation, history and dialectics. However, as distinct from the work of Küng or Schillebeeckx, who focused on biblical and doctrinal texts, Boff takes as his object of research, interpretation, history and dialectics, the new experience of Church taking place in the base Church communities.

Basic to the whole theological project is Boff's own experience of these communities (research). They pose a question, what is the meaning of this new experience? How are we to interpret this new reality (interpretation)? Are we to see this new reality as a new cutting edge for the Church, a new movement forward, or a sign of decline (history)? Finally, Boff is already aware of the diversity of opinions that exist with regard to these questions (dialectics). The area of dialectics is particularly important when Boff comes to his analysis of disputed questions. While his approach is only preliminary, the question that needs to be addressed is the root cause of this theological diversity, a variety of basic value commitments.

While the problems in these four areas dominate Boff's theology in this work, one cannot help but recognize the primary importance of the "preferential option for the poor" (conversion and foundations), for it is this which led the Brazilian Church to develop its pastoral strategy of base Church communities in the first place. Finally, there emerges out of this work an ecclesiological doctrine—a conception of Church as a communion of sisters and brothers, as church-community, church-body-of-Christ, church-people-of-God, where a basic equality takes precedence over any differentiation of function which may occur for the sake of the community (see p.27).

DISCUSSION QUESTIONS

- What role would you see for the social sciences, such as sociology and political science, in a theology of the Church? Which image best fits your understanding of the Church—a family, a body, or a society?

- What do you see as the implications of having "priestless" Christian communities?

Bibliography

As I noted above, Boff has been a prolific writer. Here I will note some of his main works.
Jesus Christ Liberator, Maryknoll, N.Y.: Orbis Books, 1978; London: SPCK, 1985—here Boff presents a liberation Christology. He draws heavily on the standard critico-historical methodology, together with some fine hermeneutical observations.
Church, Charism and Power, New York: Crossroad, 1986—a collection of essays and lectures dealing with the uses and abuses

of ecclesiastical power and its relationship to the charismatic (in the biblical sense, not the Pentecostal sense) element in the Church.

Passion of Christ—Passion of the World, Maryknoll, N.Y.: Orbis Books, 1987—here Boff presents a liberationist soteriology (theology of salvation), together with an analysis of the strengths and weaknesses of traditional soteriological models.

The Maternal Face of God, New York: Harper and Row, 1987—Boff examines the theology of Mary and seeks in it an understanding of the role of the feminine in the nature of God. While it has some good material, I found it insufficently critical in its use of masculine-feminine stereotypes.

Trinity and Society, Maryknoll, N.Y./Kent: Orbis Books/Burns & Oates, 1988—in this work, Boff examines the traditional doctrine of the Trinity. Much of the material follows classical lines in its investigation of the Trinity. It does, however, include an understanding of the Trinity from the perspective of a political, Liberation Theology.

Ecology and Liberation, Maryknoll, N.Y.: Orbis Books, 1995—this recent work, published after Boff had left the priesthood, brings liberation themes into dialogue with current ecological concerns.

Boff has also written two very good introductory works on Liberation Theology with his brother, Clodovis:

Introducing Liberation Theology, Maryknoll, N.Y./Kent: Orbis Books/Burns & Oates, 1987.

Salvation and Liberation, Maryknoll, N.Y./Melbourne: Orbis Books/Dove, 1984.

For a sympathetic treatment of Boff's conflict with the Sacred Congregation for the Doctrine of the Faith:

H. Cox, *The Silencing of Leonardo Boff*, Oak Park: Meyer Stone, 1988.

CHAPTER 15

Elisabeth Schüssler Fiorenza, *Feminist Theology I*

Feminist Theology is a very recent addition to the theological enterprise. The issue of a particularly feminist perspective in Christianity goes back to attempts in the late nineteenth and early twentieth centuries to create a "Women's Bible." The purpose of this "bible" was to delete or rewrite those sections of the Bible which were thought to be oppressive of women. Even amongst women's groups it was a controversial project. What this early attempt at a feminist critique of biblical religion made clear is that the Bible is a political book. When women sought equality of political rights, such as the right to vote, they found themselves attacked with a series of biblical texts seeking to put them in their place.

Modern Feminist Theology is, of course, much more sophisticated than that, though it is no less controversial. Feminist Theology seeks to uncover the ways in which the Christian tradition has been infected by the ideology of patriarchy. Here, patriarchy is defined as:

> ... a male pyramid of graded subordinations and exploitations [which specify] women's oppression in terms of the class, race, country, or religion of the men to whom we "belong" (p.xiv, *Bread Not Stone*).

Within patriarchy, "maleness" is defined as the norm, with women defined simply in terms of their relationships to men. Some within Feminist Theology have given up on Christianity altogether as too infected with patriarchy. Others are of a more reformist bent, seeking to challenge patriarchal structures within Christianity. Still others seek to critically reconstruct the role of women within the whole history of Christianity. This is considered necessary, since this role has been systematically repressed within the official Church stance. In order to construct a new vision for the future, one must first reconstruct and reclaim the past.

Elisabeth Schüssler Fiorenza is a key figure within Feminist Theology. Her stance is that of a critical historian seeking to discover the role of women within the history of the Church. Her principal tool is a hermeneutics of suspicion, the suspicion that the history of the Church, even as found in its foundation documents, i.e. scripture, is written from a male perspective, one which assumes a patriarchal dominance and seeks to perpetuate that dominance. Her central task is to uncover the repressed memories of the role of women in the life of the early Church.

Schüssler Fiorenza's major work to date is *In Memory of Her: A Feminist Theological Reconstruction of Christian Origins*. It is a difficult but probing book on the history of the early Church. Its difficulty lies in its attempts to "read the silences" (i.e. the gaps in information about women), the breadth of its sources and the imaginative leaps the author is forced to take, justifiable but still controversial. Schüssler Fiorenza draws on a wealth of historical information about the Biblical, Greek and Roman worlds, especially on the place and role of women within these worlds. In many ways, it is a work for specialists. However, she has also had published a collection of essays, *Bread Not Stone*, for a more popular audience, and it is on these that we shall focus.

In many ways, Feminist Theology, like Liberation Theology and Political Theology, is based on an ideology critique. Here the ideology under attack is patriarchy. As such, Feminist Theology calls for a conversion, an option, not for the poor as in Liberation Theology, but away from the patterns of domination and marginalization that patriarchy creates. Inasmuch as these patterns are found within the Church and its history, then conversion is necessary. In this way Feminist Theology is quite different from Liberation and Political theologies. While they tend to seek out and expose ideologies which justify economic and social realities in "the world," Feminist Theology focuses its attention squarely on ideological distortions operative within Church teachings and practice. This radical stance can be both threatening and liberating to those who identify with the Church and its traditions.

Material under consideration—*Bread Not Stone*,[1] Boston: Beacon Press, 1984

As was mentioned above, the book *Bread Not Stone* is a collection of essays, exploring the questions raised by a feminist interpretation of the Bible. As is often the case with such collections, there tends to be a repetition of key themes, placed together in different constellations, reworked for different occasions. This being the case, I intend to focus on the first two essays, as these give a good overall impression of the contents of the total work. They also raise the basic methodological issues present in Feminist Theology. In fact, most of the essays in this work deal with methodological issues. For actual application of this methodology to particular texts and traditions, one should consider the more substantial work, *In Memory of Her*.

The first essay, "Women-Church," examines the response of the feminist movement to "biblical religion." As Schüssler Fiorenza points out, feminist studies have called into question a male-dominated academy which has marginalized women and the contributions of women to history. In all areas of historical studies, feminist scholars have sought to recover the contributions of women, contributions which have often been neglected or slighted by a focus on male achievements. She argues that this same approach now needs to be applied to biblical and other early Christian texts. This will involve a shift from an androcentric (i.e. male-centered) framework, of texts written by men and interpreted by men, to a feminist interpretative framework. Within this framework the:

> ... heuristic key is not a dual theological anthropology of masculine and feminine, or the concept of the complementarity of the sexes, or a metaphysical principle of female ascendency. Its

formulations are based on the radical assumption that gender is socially, politically, economically, and theologically constructed and that such a social construction serves to perpetuate the patriarchal exploitation and oppression of all women, which is most fully expressed in the fate of the "poorest and most despised women on earth" (p.7).

Rather than use the poor as its "hermeneutical center," as we find in Liberation Theology, Feminist Theology finds its hermeneutical center in "women-church," a movement of self-identified women and women-identified men, whose commitment and mission is one of solidarity with women suffering the triple oppressions of sexism, racism and poverty. It is women's experience of oppression and marginalization which grants their experience this privileged hermeneutic status. To adopt such a center of hermeneutic privilege is obviously to call into question Church structures which are commonly dominated by men and which tend to exclude women from any meaningful participation.

The question that Schüssler Fiorenza then addresses is: what sort of stand does "women-church" take with regard to the Bible? Can the Bible be a book for women-church, or is it irredeemably patriarchal, a product of a patriarchal age seeking to maintain patriarchy? In this regard, many feminists do regard biblical religion as irredeemably patriarchal and so have abandoned biblical religion. Many in the "moral majority" would agree, for there is a long history of the Bible being used against feminists in their struggle for political, social, economic and religious rights. As Political Theology alerts us, such biblical fundamentalism is not without its own political intent.

Among feminists who remain within Christian circles, some have sought to recover biblical religion, seeking a "usable past." Schüssler Fiorenza outlines the various strategies which have been used in this recovery process. One is the apologetic recovery, which seeks to explain how various texts have been misunderstood or misused. Reference is made to the context and the cultural limitations of the text, to explain away difficult texts. Here, both feminist apologists and conservatives use biblical texts to forward their own stance. Schüssler Fiorenza criticizes both for using the text as a "mythical archetype" which "establishes an ideal form for all times, an unchanging pattern of behavior and theological structure for the community" (p.10). For example, those who oppose the ordination of women argue that since Jesus only allowed men to be present at the Last Supper, only men can be priests.

Within this strategy of apologetic recovery, Schüssler Fiorenza discerns three approaches. One is the doctrinal model, which seeks to argue either for or against the oppression of women by direct reference to biblical texts. A second approach, the historical-factual approach, tends to identify biblical truth and authority with historical or textual factualness. Thus, critico-historical methods are used to discern texts and traditions as historically reliable and these are then taken as normative. Finally, there is what she calls the dialogical-pluralistic approach, which sees texts and traditions as theological responses of communities to their own historical circumstances. This approach recognizes a variety of stances within the sources, even contradictory stances, but then seeks to determine a "canon within the canon," some principle within the sources themselves, which then becomes the hermeneutical key for all interpretation. (The most famous "canon within the canon" approach was that of Luther, who made "justification by faith alone" the hermeneutical key for the interpretation of scripture.)

As an alternative, Schüssler Fiorenza proposes the use of the Bible as an "historical prototype," not something that establishes unchanging forms, but one which uncovers a prototype, a first model, which all others are related to in a critical way. Here inspired truth is limited to "matters pertaining to the salvation, freedom and liberation of all, especially women" (p.14). Inasmuch as it fails this "test," it is not taken to be inspired. Thus we can see the significance of women-church as a hermeneutic center for Feminist Theology. For it is the present experience, in the present political situation which, in part, determines the "inspiration" of the text. So, if asked the question I posed in Chapter 4—is something revealed because it is experienced as salvific or is it salvific because it is revealed?— Schüssler Fiorenza would reply that it is revealed inasmuch as it is experienced as salvific and liberating. Thus, any text which is used to oppress loses its authority as inspired.

Within this framework, the Bible becomes not an authoritative source but a resource for recovering the liberating impulse of God's action in the world. Part of what is to be recovered is the *memoria passionis*, the memory of the suffering of women within the biblical tradition:

> This heritage is misrepresented when it is understood solely as a history of patriarchal oppression; it must also be reconstituted as a history of liberation and religious agency. The history and theology of women's oppression perpetuated by patriarchal biblical texts and clerical patriarchy must be understood for what they are. The history and theology must not be allowed to cancel out the memory of struggle, life and leadership of biblical women who spoke and acted in the power of the Spirit (p.20).

In the second essay, "For the Sake of our Salvation ... ," Schüssler Fiorenza spells out in more detail the various paradigms which she argues are used to provide interpretative frameworks for scripture.

Firstly, there is the doctrinal paradigm which sees scripture as the word of God, conceived in ahistorical, dogmatic terms. This is similar to Dulles' first model, revelation as doctrine, considered in Chapter 4. Within this model, scripture simply has the task of providing proof texts—all arguments are settled by "scripture says, therefore ... ."

Secondly, there is the historical paradigm, the Bible as a book of the past. Here, only that which can be critically appropriated from the past is seen as authoritative (cf. Dulles' revelation as history model). It seeks a purely "objective" reconstruction of the facts and these then become normative, e.g. if Jesus excluded women from the Last Supper then there can be no women priests! This model is the dominant model used in scriptural studies. Its critico-historical method treats scripture not as canonical texts for a community of faith, but as "historical religious documents of Judaism and Christianity in antiquity" (p.30).

The use of this historical model creates tension within the Church community since, while ministers are trained within this model, the hierarchy (and most laity) still operate in the doctrinal model. Moreover, Schüssler Fiorenza argues that the "value-neutral" exegesis that this model proposes as the ideal fails to recognize that we come to the scriptures with a prior faith commitment. Ministers trained in such a model are then left to their own devices to bridge the gap between the value-neutral exegesis of the academy and communities seeking nourishment for their faith commitment. While the critico-historical method attempts to discover what the text meant, the minister is left to struggle over what the text means, here and now, for his or her community.

Finally, there is the pastoral theological paradigm. Here:

> . . . biblical interpretation cannot limit itself to working out what the author meant; it must also critically elaborate what the theological significance of the text is for today. . . . (I)t understands the Bible, not as a conglomeration of doctrinal propositions or proofs, not as historical-factual transcripts, but as a model of Christian life and faith (p.32).

Indeed, Schüssler Fiorenza argues that this is how the Biblical texts understand themselves. They do not seek to present doctrinal propositions or historical diaries, but rather seek to promote and encourage Christian life and faith within their own concrete pastoral situation.

> The New Testament authors rewrote their traditions in the forms of letters, gospels, or apocalypses, because they felt theologically compelled to illuminate or censure the beliefs and praxis of their communities. The biblical books are thus written with the intention of serving the needs of the community of faith and not of revealing timeless principles or transmitting historically accurate records (p.35).

Thus, to Schüssler Fiorenza, an essential part of the process of scriptural interpretation and preaching is the present context of the audience. Just as the biblical authors rewrote their traditions in the light of the context of their own communities, so we must "rewrite" them in the light of our own context. Within our own context, those texts may take on a new meaning, for example as oppressive of women, which requires a critical response from the interpreter or preacher.

Schüssler Fiorenza here places herself in what she sees as a Catholic tradition, which sees scripture not as revelation but as containing revelation (cf. the *Dogmatic Constitution on Divine Revelation*, Vatican II). What is important within the scriptures is what is there for the "sake of our salvation." However, salvation in not an abstract reality, concerned with my soul, but a concrete reality of liberation from the many forces of sin and evil which are oppressing me in the present situation. Hence, Schüssler Fiorenza argues, it is only within the Christian community, where such salvation is being experienced, that the biblical texts can be interpreted. Only such communities can provide criteria for discerning the salvific content of the scripture in the present situation. Texts which are used to oppress and destroy freedom cannot claim a divine mandate.

> For example, feminist theology has pointed out that women are oppressed and exploited by patriarchal and sexist structures and institutions. Therefore, according to this criterion, biblical revelation and truth can today be found only in those texts and traditions that transcend and criticize the patriarchal culture and religion of their times (p.41).

Such a pastoral-theological approach will find revelation only in the non-sexist traditions of the Church.

Again we see here the importance of women-church as a hermeneutic center. It is within women-church that the experience of salvation from patriarchy is had, so that it is only within women-church that the liberating word of God can be interpreted. Unless one has been freed from the ideological distortion of patriarchy, one's interpretation must always be suspected of at least implicitly supporting patriarchal structures of domination. Such a stance radically calls into question our whole theological project.

In summary, the following needs to be said. Feminist Theology cannot simply be reduced to an indirect way of arguing for women priests, though that is clearly one issue which it seeks to open up. It is much more than this. It seeks to uncover the ways in which gender identification, sex role stereotypes and patriarchal assumptions have operated in ways to marginalize, and justify the marginalization of, women throughout

Christian history. At its heart lies what it sees as an authentic Christian vision of a community of equals, with neither Jew nor Gentile, neither slave nor free, neither male nor female (cf. Galatians 3:28). As such, it poses questions which traditional theology has been slow to recognize.

Comments on theological method

It is interesting, in these methodological notes, to compare the position of Schüssler Fiorenza with that of Lonergan, which we have been using in our previous analyses.

Schüssler Fiorenza rejects the critico-historical method as incomplete in its approach to the interpretation of scripture. Such a method fails to make explicit the fact that the texts arise out of a faith commitment and are interpreted within a faith context. The method's "value-free" approach is contradicted by this context. In the same way, Lonergan completes the tasks of research, interpretation and history (the main components of the critico-historical method) with the task of dialectics. Dialectics identifies the value commitments of the interpreter as the source of diversity in the results of the critico-historical phase.

Both Lonergan and Schüssler Fiorenza then locate conversion at the heart of the theological project. For Schüssler Fiorenza, conversion is located in "women-church," the movement of self-identified women and women-identified men, who have experienced a conversion away from patriarchy as a form of human oppression. In the light of this conversion, dialectics becomes both a hermeneutics of suspicion against patriarchy and a hermeneutics of recovery seeking to uncover a "usable past" for women. For Lonergan, conversion brings faith, which involves a turning away from the irrationalities of dehumanizing and depersonalizing social and historical bias. Clearly, patriarchy can be seen as an example of such a dehumanizing and depersonalizing bias.

However, while Lonergan can see the possibility of the formulation of doctrines out of the foundational experience of conversion, Schüssler Fiorenza, at least on the explicit level, does not want to speak about doctrines as permanent statements of the Church's understanding of salvation. To her, such statements are always culturally relative—there are no timeless principles revealed to the Church.

Without being too critical, I would see a tension in Schüssler Fiorenza's position on this matter. As I noted above, there lies at the heart of Feminist Theology a vision of authentic Christian community as a community of equals, neither Jew nor Gentile, neither free nor slave, neither male nor female. This vision arises out of the conversion experience, which identifies and rejects patriarchy and which is foundational for Feminist Theology. One could claim that it is transcultural, since it acts as a critique of any cultural ideology of domination. To all intents and purposes, it acts as a doctrine within women-church.

These methodological points should not detract from what has been achieved in Feminist Theology. As an ideological critique of patriarchy as expressed within the Church, it has the power to sensitize us to issues which would otherwise be lost in the male-dominated theological academy. It will be of great interest to see how the Church reacts to and eventually integrates the positive contribution that Feminist Theology has to make.

DISCUSSION QUESTIONS

- How would you see the relationship between feminism and Christianity? Is a Christian feminism or a feminist Christianity possible?

- How would you approach scriptural texts which seem to be oppressive of women?

Bibliography

Schüssler Fiorenza's first major work in English was:
In Memory of Her, New York: Crossroad, 1984—a detailed study of the role of women in the early Church, together with a significant methodological contribution in Part I. This is basically a specialist work, difficult but rewarding.

Since then she has also had published the following major works:

Discipleship of Equals: A Critical Feminist Ekklesia-logy of Liberation, New York/London: Crossroad/SCM, 1993—this is a collection of occasional essays in the general area of feminist ecclesiology. Its fundamental starting-point is that the Church exists as a community of equals so that hierarchical structures are counter to the Church's true nature.

Jesus: Miriam's Child, Sophia's Prophet, New York/London: Continuum/SCM, 1994—here Schüssler Fiorenza develops a feminist Christology, with special emphasis on the Wisdom (Sophia) influence on the authors of the New Testament. The work also contains significant feminist reflection on the place of Mary in Christian faith, deconstructing some of the "high" Mariology which once dominated the Catholic imagination.

For further works on Feminist Theology, see the next chapter.

---

1. Since the first edition of *Introducing Contemporary Theologies*, Schüssler Fiorenza's book *Bread Not Stone* has been republished in a new edition.

CHAPTER 16

Rosemary Radford Ruether, *Feminist Theology II*

Rosemary Radford Ruether is another leading figure in the area of Feminist Theology. While her recent writings have been in this area, it has not always been her key concern. In a theological career stretching over twenty years, her initial interest had been more in the area of Liberation Theology and the interaction between theology and social issues. Her interest in feminist issues grew out of her larger commitment to the concerns of human liberation—racism, militarism, economic exploitation, anti-Semitism. Indeed, in the sixties she was involved both in anti-Vietnam war demonstrations and in the civil rights movement. In taking up Feminist Theology, Ruether was following lines of thought already well developed in dealing with other areas of oppression.

While her initial training was in the humanities and history (she has written, for example, a scholarly work on an early Father of the Church, *Gregor of Nazianzus: Rhetor and Philosopher*), most of her writings deal with contemporary social issues and broad theological themes. She has written a work on Liberation Theology entitled *Liberation Theology: Human Hope Confronts Christian History and American Power*, and one on anti-Semitism: *Faith and Fratricide: The Theological Roots of Anti-semitism*. Her specifically feminist works deal with Christology, creation, liturgy, Church structure and practice—the whole range of Christian life and theory reevaluated in the light of a Feminist Theology.

Apart from her books, Ruether has maintained a high public profile through her regular contributions to the American

Catholic newspaper, *National Catholic Reporter*. She is also well known for her public stand on abortion law reform and her membership of Catholics for a Free Choice. Such a stand, radically at variance with traditional Catholic moral teaching, should not distract us from the positive theological contribution her work makes. Ruether's theology forces us to ask questions and face up to answers which many would rather ignore. A faithful theology must be willing to address all questions, lest in the final analysis it fall over into fideism.

Material under consideration—*Sexism and God-Talk*,[1] Boston: Beacon Press, 1983

The work *Sexism and God-Talk* is an initial attempt by Ruether to write a systematic Feminist Theology. The work of Schüssler Fiorenza, which we considered earlier, was basically concerned with the methodological issues which a Feminist Theology raises, particularly with regard to the exegesis of scripture. Ruether, on the other hand, is here seeking to develop a systematic account of major theological themes, such as Christology, creation, Mariology, ecclesiology and eschatology.

In her examination of various theological themes, the basic assumption is that the theological tradition has been infected by patriarchy, and that the various theological themes have been developed in such a way as to keep women in inferior positions, both in society and in the Church. Thus, the doctrine of creation was used to justify the claim that the dominance of male over female was part of God's created order. In Christology, the maleness of Jesus was used to bolster the notion of maleness being normative, and female being secondary and derivative. Moreover, Jesus' maleness is used as an argument to deny women's access to ordained ministry. Mary becomes the ideal type of female submissiveness which women are exhorted to imitate. Failing that, they become Eve, the temptress, the seductress, leading men into sin.

Behind these theological traditions, Ruether identifies an anthropology which sees maleness as the normative definition of what it means to be human, with femaleness being secondary and inferior. She finds that Augustine, while affirming that men possess the image of God, denied that women possess that same image of God:

> .... but when she is referred separately in her quality as a help-meet, which regards the woman alone, then she is not the image of God, but as regards the male alone, he is the image of God as fully and completely as when the woman too is joined within him in one (*De Trinitate* 7.7.10, quoted on p.95).

Similarly, Aquinas saw women, even in the created order, as defective and servile to men. He believed that, by nature, women have less rational capacity and are less capable of moral self-control. The Fall compounds this situation! While Luther recognized the possibility that in the original order of creation women and men may have been equal, he held that, in the fallen state, women's subjugation is a fitting punishment for Eve's part in our original sin. Thus, male domination of women can be theologically justified! Even the twentieth-century Protestant theologian, Karl Barth, justifies the domination of male over female, though for him it is part of the divine order of creation.

It is not difficult to see the political implications of such theological stances. These are not primarily theological statements, but ideological ones, used to justify and maintain patterns of male domination over women. Running parallel to these traditions, Ruether also uncovers minority traditions which have sought to establish a more egalitarian anthropology asserting the basic equality of male and female. She draws on the work of Elisabeth Schüssler Fiorenza, who has uncovered an "egalitarian counter-cultural trend" within early Christianity, often associated with mystical sects and movements later condemned as heretical, e.g. the Gnostics. In more recent history, the same egalitarian position can be found in sects such as the Quakers and the Shakers.

Ruether identifies other anthropologies which attempt to analyze human existence using categories of male and female. Liberal feminism will take its stand on the equality of rights between and capacities of men and women. Ruether notes that liberal feminism has been one of the prime movers in seeking recognized ministry for women. However, she is critical of liberal feminism's failure to question underlying structures of society and Church. It "too readily identifies normative human nature with those capacities for reason and rule identified with men and with the public sphere" (p.109). On the other hand, it does proclaim the truth that women do, in fact, have equal capacities to men in these areas.

Ruether also identifies romantic feminism, in its conservative, reformist and radical forms. These put forward a notion of female supremacy, that women are morally superior to men. For conservatives, this means the promotion of home and family, the women's moral sphere. For reformists, this means taking those female moral values into society to change it for the better, e.g. if women ruled there would be no more wars! Finally, for radical feminism, the only solution to male contamination is a separate female society which totally excludes men.

Ruether is also critical of romantic feminism. It is quite correct, she claims, in identifying virtues relegated to women as clues to a better society. However, it fails to recognize that these virtues, as practiced in society at present, "exist in deformed and deforming ways within the institutionalization of 'woman's sphere'" (p.110).

In the light of these criticisms, what is needed, claims Ruether, is an anthropology which recognizes all humans as possessing "full and equivalent human nature and personhood, as male and female" (p.111). Such a position takes its stand not on natural, biological or psychic accounts of what is male or female. It takes its stand on a recognition that male and female roles, apart from the most basic biological roles of generation, are primarily of social origin. They are a way of ordering society, and any anthropology which ignores this becomes, in the end, an ideological justification for that ordering. In seeking to overcome the ontological dualism of such ideologies, "women want to tear down the walls that separate the self and society into 'male' and 'female' spheres. This demands not just a new integrated self but a new integrated social order" (p.113).

This anthropological position then becomes the starting point for Ruether's investigation of the various theological themes considered in her book. Can a male savior save women? Is Mary a symbol of women's repression or their liberation? Is sexism our original sin? What are the forms of ministry appropriate in a Church freed from patriarchy? What is the vision of society generated by a non-sexist anthropology? What claims can be made concerning our future life, our "stake in immortality"? Clearly we cannot hope to consider all these issues. I intend therefore to focus on the material dealing with our consciousness of evil, sexism and original sin (Chapter 7).

In a chapter entitled "The Consciousness of Evil: The Journeys of Conversion," Ruether examines the nature of sexism as evil, as part of our human "original sinfulness," and the process of conversion away from this evil. Ruether notes that it is only in the experience of conversion that we are able to identify evil as evil. Thus, feminism, which involves a conversion away from patriarchy, "represents a fundamental shift in the valuations of good and evil" (p.160). Such a conversion involves a recognition that sin is not just individual, but includes a disruption of human community:

> Feminism continues, in a new form, the basic Christian perception that sin, as perversion of good potential into evil, is not simply individual but refers to a fallen state of humanity (p.161).

From this perspective, sexism is part of our original human sinfulness, an expression of the fundamental brokenness in human relations, whereby the self-other relationship is distorted into a good-evil, superior-inferior dualism. Patterns of cooperation and sharing are replaced by patterns of domination and control. Sexism, which sees male-female relationship in terms of a good-evil, superior-inferior dualism, of male dominating female, is a primary example of such distortion.

Ruether gives examples from Jewish, Christian and Greek mythology which express this distortion of relationship into dualism—Lilith, Eve, Pandora. She sees these as a mythologizing of early infancy where the mother provides for all the child's needs. The myths then scapegoat women, as mothers, for the loss of this paradise from which the child is wrenched into the adult (male) world of harsh struggle. These myths:

> . . . translate female evil into an ontological principle. The female

comes to represent the qualities of materiality, irrationality, carnality, and finitude, which debase the "manly" spirit and drag it down into sin and death (p.169).

Once one begins to recognize that this dualism has more to do with the projection of repressed and negative aspects of the male psyche than with female evil, once one begins to recognize that sexism is in fact evil, then the whole structure of patriarchy begins to crumble. "Every aspect of male privilege loses its authority as natural and divine right and is reevaluated as sin and evil" (p.173). Ruether notes that, for women, this can be a shattering experience. Not only does it arouse suspicion in relation to their most intimate relations, with husband, children, fathers, but it also arouses a guilt within themselves for their own acquiescence in and perpetuation of a system of male domination.

To recognize sexism as sin is not to label men as naturally more evil or immoral than women. This would be the romantic feminism option that Ruether has already rejected. Both men and women have the capacity to sin. However, this recognition should not blind us to the fact that historically men have been more responsible for evil in the world:

> The monopolization of power and privilege by ruling class males also means a monopolization of the opportunities for evil. This means not only that men have been the primary decision-makers of history but also that the very modes of relationship set up by this monopoly of power and privilege create violent and oppressive ways of pursuing the "good ends" envisioned by this male ruling class (p.180).

Again, such a position does not imply that any individual male should carry the total burden of guilt for sexism. All men and women carry some guilt, either through enjoying its benefits or through their acquiescence in its oppression. Sexism so permeates society as to shape our imagination, our consciousness, from our earliest days. "Long before we can even begin to make our own decisions, we are already thoroughly its product" (p.182).

Ruether takes us on a journey of conversion away from

sexism, looking at how conversion affects both women and men. For women in general it is a difficult task, challenging and breaking out of traditional female roles which they have long been socialized to accept. For Christian women it is often even more difficult. A male-defined theology has long identified sin with anger and pride. Virtue, on the other hand, was identified with "feminine" traits of humility and self-denial.

In identifying sexism as sin, women experience a deep anger. But this is not a destructive anger. It is a righteous anger, a prophetic anger, at an injustice long perpetrated. Such an anger is a "liberating grace," which empowers women to break the chains of sexist socialization. Further, women begin to develop a sense of their own worth, a new sense of pride, a basic self-esteem. Again, this is not the pride condemned by male moralists, but a basic self-esteem necessary for one's own identity. "Without basic self-esteem one has no self at all, as a base upon which to build an identity or to criticize past mistakes" (p.186).

The male journey of conversion is, of course, different. Initially, men tend to be dismissive, trivializing the matter, with claims that women benefit from sexist structures as much as men do. If they can get beyond this, the next stage recognizes the reality of sexist oppression, but claims that men suffer from it as much as women, since they have been forced to suppress their own "feminine" side. They are in as much need of liberation as women. They draw on the Jungian terminology of anima-animus to provide a metaphysical framework to justify their claims. For Ruether, however:

> . . . these two stances are not conversion, but ways of resisting conversion. . . . Real conversion from sexism begins to happen only when a man is able to enter into real solidarity with women in the struggle for liberation, often by being involved in a relationship with a particular woman who is pursuing her own liberation. By entering into her struggle, seeing the world of sexism from her eyes, he begins to be able to understand some dimensions of sexism (pp.190–191).

As with any conversion, there is a price to pay. For men, it may mean scorn from the male group ego, loss of economic status and privilege, breaking away from long-accustomed roles and ways of relating. However, such a price is a small one to pay in order to regain humanity for women and men.

As an aside, it is interesting to note how the Church has gone through the first two of these stages in relation to priesthood for women. Traditional arguments were simply that women were inferior, that in fact they benefited from male domination and so could not be priests . Modern arguments are more of the "equal but different" type. Men and women have equal but complementary roles to play. Men have the role of leadership, women have different complementary roles—again, women cannot be priests. As Ruether notes, both stages are ways of resisting conversion.

Comments on theological method

As we noted in the previous chapter, the main theological method of Feminist Theology is a hermeneutic of suspicion, a suspicion that the Christian tradition is infected by patriarchy. Whereas Fiorenza concentrated on the methodological implications of such a procedure, especially in interpreting scripture, Ruether has turned this hermeneutic to work on major theological themes, pointing out the way in which theological traditions have been used to support, and in some cases, have been built upon, patriarchal assumptions.

Ruether draws her inspiration from the biblical prophetic tradition. It is the prophetic principle of questioning the patterns of domination and oppression operative within society and calling for justice to reign that she sees as a major resource for Feminist Theology. This prophetic principle becomes her "canon-within-the-canon" (note, a position rejected on methodological grounds by Schüssler Fiorenza). Feminism radicalizes this biblical tradition by its recognition of sexism as a major pattern of domination and oppression.

As with the political theology of Metz, we see here the close connection between the two functional specialities of dialectics and foundations, swinging on the hinge of conversion. Dialectics analyzes the different value stances which ground different interpretations of reality. Conversion identifies which are values, which disvalues. As Ruether notes, it is out of the conversion experience that one can identify evil as evil. As we noted above, feminism involves "a fundamental shift in the valuations of good and evil" (p.160). The foundational task is then to name the evil, to identify its manifold implications, and to denounce it. This is the task of a hermeneutic of suspicion.

However, a one-sided hermeneutic of suspicion has its dangers. While it is true that the theological tradition has been used to support patriarchy, it does not necessarily follow that this tradition has been based on patriarchal assumptions. A hermeneutic of suspicion often needs to be followed by a hermeneutic of recovery, one which can recover the positive values which the tradition sought to transmit. Can one simply dismiss, as Ruether does in her chapter on eschatology, the question of personal existence after death as largely a male problem, "an effort to absolutize personal or individual ego as itself everlasting, over against the total community of being" (p.257)? Could it not also be seen as a hope for universal justice? Other masters of the hermeneutic of suspicion, Freud and Marx, found themselves unable to affirm anything noble about human existence, reducing everything to base psychic or economic motives. I feel Ruether runs the same risk.

Such a negative comment should not, however, detract from the contribution that Ruether makes in her work. A hermeneutic of suspicion has its place, and is at its best in seeking to uncover real evil. However, evil is a dangerous thing—as Ruether notes, one may "risk going a bit mad" in seeking to "understand the depths of the evil of sexism" (p.187). Ruether helps us to understand some of those depths and face up to the ways in which we have been complicit in that evil.

DISCUSSION QUESTIONS

● In your opinion has Christianity done more to harm or help women in the quest for equality? Give examples of both if possible.

● From your own experience how accurate is Ruether's account of conversion away from sexism?

Bibliography

Apart from the books already mentioned in the opening section of this chapter, the following are significant works by Ruether:
The Radical Kingdom: The Western Experience of Messianic Hopes, New York: Paulist Press, 1970—an analysis of the socio-political impact of the scriptural message in view of the decline of Western liberalism.
New Woman New Earth: Sexist Ideologies and Human Liberation, New York: Seabury Press, 1975—Ruether's first work on feminism. It seeks to integrate feminist thought with other themes of human liberation.
Women-Church: Theology and Practice of Feminist Liturgical Communities, New York: Harper and Row, 1985—a theoretical and practical handbook for the women-church movement. Ruether gives both a theological backing and practical liturgical structures and rites for Women-Church.
Gaia and God, San Franciso: HarperCollins, 1992—this work weaves feminist concerns into the ecological debate, seeing the present state of the environment as a further symptom of patriarchy. It analyzes the contribution of Western Christianity to our ecological problems and considers the resources the Christian tradition can bring to bear in healing the world.

For a readable account of the role of women in the early Church, and an analysis of the human experience underlying that role:
R. Haughton, *The Re-Creation of Eve*, Illinois: Templegate, 1985.

---

1. Since the first edition of *Introducing Contemporary Theologies*, Ruether's book *Sexism and God-Talk* has been reissued in a tenth anniversary edition.

CHAPTER 17

Elizabeth Johnson, *Feminist Theology III*

Elisabeth Schüssler Fiorenza and Rosemary Radford Ruether were pioneers in the task of bringing contemporary feminism into active dialogue with contemporary theology. Fiorenza brought a critique of patriarchy to bear on Christianity's foundational documents, the Scriptures. She helped uncover the silences in the text, the ways in which women were made invisible by the patriarchal perspective of its authors. Ruether brought the same critique to bear on the doctrinal and theological tradition of Christianity, uncovering the biases against women to be found in that tradition. Their groundbreaking works opened up the field for constructive and substantial dialogue, reflection and debate on the role of woman in the Church, the nature of sexism, and the way Christianity has lost its original thrust as a "community of equals." In many ways the work of Elizabeth Johnson marks a profound maturing of this debate.

Johnson would hardly strike one as a radical figure. She is a Catholic nun working in a well-reputed Catholic university. Moreover her books and articles reflect a profound, if critical, respect for the Catholic tradition. There is no knee-jerk rejection of figures from the past, such as Augustine and Aquinas, because of their obvious patriarchal bias. Rather there is a critical retrieval of their positive insights, and the active utilization of these insights within a developing feminist perspective. Still, her work is deeply unsettling in the biases she uncovers and the strategies she develops to overcome them. Johnson makes no apology for her constant references to God as "She," a move she sees as necessary to help liberate our imaginations from centuries of patriarchal domination. Coming at a time when the Catholic Church would not sanction a gender-inclusive English translation of the new *Catechism of the Catholic Church*, such a strategy is bound to upset some.

Johnson has not produced as yet a large body of work—only a few books and several learned articles. However, the work we shall be considering, *She Who Is: The Mystery of God in Feminist Theological Discourse*, has been extraordinarily well received. It is a mature work which demands respect, even from those who may not agree with her approach.

Work under consideration—*She Who Is: The Mystery of God in Feminist Theological Discourse*, New York: Crossroad, 1993

If there is one issue which dominates this work it is the question of how to speak properly about God. The religious tradition of humanity has presented us with a variety of images, symbols, concepts and judgments which seek to mediate something of the divine mystery to human experience. Yet within the Christian experience certain symbols have become dominant, those which speak of God, especially the trinitarian God, in male terms. What is a feminist theology to make of this? Are male symbols the only ones adequate to represent divinity? Are women, too, *imago Dei*, made in the image of God, and hence capable of representing God? Or are female symbols forever excluded from such God-talk? The answers to these questions are not only saying something about men and women, but ultimately they are saying something about God. As Johnson questions:

> What is the right way to speak about God in the face of women's newly cherished human dignity and equality? This is a crucial theological question. What is at stake is the truth about God, inseparable from the situation of human beings, and the identity and mission of the faith community itself (p.6).

Part of feminism's new experience of women's dignity is the assertion that women are indeed made in the image of God, something that the theological tradition has been unable to accept (see, for example, the chapter on Ruether). From this perspective the dominance of male symbols is judged to be both oppressive and idolatrous. It is oppressive because it legitimates patriarchal structures and relegates women and children to the margins. It is idolatrous in that the exclusively used male-dominated language "absolutizes a single set of metaphors and obscures the height and depth and length and breadth of divine mystery" (p.18).

To this extent the tradition is infected with a bias against the genuine humanity of women, not simply at a superficial level but at its depths. What is needed to overcome this bias, argues Johnson, are new non-hierarchical models of relationship, models which are inclusive and celebratory of difference, rather than exclusive of women and suspicious of difference. She concedes that the problem does not lie in the use of male symbols for God, since men too are made in the image of God. "Rather, the problem consists in the fact that these male terms are used exclusively, literally, and patriarchally" (p.33). As Johnson regularly repeats, "the symbol of God functions"; it is never simply ideologically neutral. It can function to promote good or to undermine it. Religious symbols in particular are double-edged, since in pointing to the divine, we run the risk of making the finite symbols an idol. Then the symbol loses its symbolic and evocative character and "divine mystery is cramped into a fixed, petrified image" (p.39).

How then to speak of God in term of female symbols? Many theologians, not only feminists, have struggled with this question. Some have spoken of feminine traits or dimensions of God. It is not uncommon to hear male theologians speak of God's compassion and tenderness as a "feminine" traits. However Johnson does not find this approach adequate. God remains basically "He," with feminine traits to soften "His" image. Androcentrism is unaffected. Also the very notion of feminine and masculine traits is a socially constructed stereotype which in itself can function to subordinate women. Thus, Johnson concludes, this approach does not, in the end, liberate women.

Others have attempted to speak of the Holy Spirit as the

feminine dimension of God. Leonardo Boff is a notable example in his work, *The Maternal Face of God*. However, this approach flounders on the same rock of stereotypical assumptions about what is masculine and what is feminine (though often justified by reference to the psychology of Carl Jung). Also the language of "dimensions" is difficult to align with traditional theologies of God's Being. God cannot be parceled out into bits or dimensions.

As an alternative, Johnson proposes that both male and female images of God are equally valid and equally problematic. "The mystery of God transcends all images but can be spoken about equally well and poorly in concepts taken from male and female reality" (p.56). Notwithstanding this, Johnson makes an explicit option to speak of God in almost exclusively female terms:

> Until a strong measure of undervalued female symbolism is introduced and used with ease, equivalent imaging of God male and female, which I myself have advocated and still hold to be a goal, remains an abstraction, expressive of an ideal but unrealizable in actual life (p.57).

Thus throughout her book Johnson refers to God as "She" and "her."

Johnson further justifies this approach by drawing upon the Scriptures and the theological tradition of Christianity. In both she uncovers resources which can assist in her project. In the Scriptures she finds ample references to God in female terms, most notably in the symbol of Sophia/Wisdom. She understands Biblical references to Sophia not as a feminine "dimension" of the divine, not as a divine intermediary between God and creation, but simply as God spoken of in female terms. From the theological tradition she recovers the sense of divine incomprehensibility, so that no image, no symbol is adequate to the divine. Further, Scholasticism developed the *via analogia*, the analogical way of speaking about God. Given that women too are *imago Dei*, proper analogies from women's reality can be found for the divine. Such an analogical approach, however, must always keep in mind that any similarity posited must take into account an even greater dissimilarity! And this applies to both male and female images of God.

Having uncovered these resources Johnson turns her attention to the classical doctrine of the Trinity. Rather than beginning with God the "Father" and then moving onto the "Son" and Spirit, Johnson reverses the order, beginning with an account of the Holy Spirit, who is first in terms of human experience. She speaks of the Spirit as Spirit-Sophia, then speaks of Jesus as Jesus-Sophia, divine Wisdom incarnate, and the first person of the Trinity as Mother-Sophia. Now there is a relatively long, if minor, tradition of speaking of the Spirit in female terms, and one can easily accept that the first person of the Trinity is in fact neither male nor female, and so that Father and Mother are equally adequate symbols to denote this person. However, as Johnson recognizes, and does not call into doubt, historically Jesus was male. How then does a feminist theology deal with the maleness of Jesus? In particular, as Ruether before her has asked, can a male savior save women?

Johnson begins by acknowledging the feminist critique which argues that Jesus' maleness has been used to provide a sacred justification for male dominance and female subordination. Indeed it has served "as a religious tool for marginalizing and excluding women" (p.151). The maleness of Jesus has been used to reinforce a patriarchal image of God, implying that somehow maleness is an essential characteristic of divinity. This then spills over into an androcentric anthropology where a special divine dignity accrues to the male sex by means of its "natural resemblance" to God. Johnson argues that if this stance is pushed then, at least implicitly, women's salvation is put at risk. Evoking the classical Christological axiom, "what is not assumed is not saved," she notes that if maleness is somehow an essential characteristic of Jesus' salvific work, then "female humanity is not assumed and therefore not saved" (p.153). This is the risk of an androcentric Christology.

As an alternative to the polar anthropology of male-female, Johnson proposed a multipolar approach which takes in humanity in all its concreteness. Not just sexual identity, but also racial, social, economic, political and cultural poles are constitutive of human existence. Sexuality is just one factor in the boundless diversity of concrete human existence, a diversity which is not a threat but a resource for building true human community.

Turning to the actual praxis of Jesus, Johnson draws attention to the liberating quality of his ministry:

> Through his ministry Jesus unleashes a hope, a vision, and a present experience of liberating relationships that women, the lowest of the low in any class, as well as men, savor as the antithesis of patriarchy. Women interact with Jesus in mutual respect, support, comfort and challenge . . . (p.157).

Jesus' fidelity to this ministry of liberation eventually leads to his state execution. Jesus does not die because God requires it but because of his solidarity with the suffering and lost. Paradoxically, in reflecting on this mystery of redemption, Johnson identifies an appropriateness about Jesus' maleness. Here she follows a Scholastic approach which argues that certain matters pertaining to redemption are fitting, appropriate, though not necessary. If a woman had propounded the message of Jesus, "she most certainly would have been greeted with a colossal shrug" (p.160). It is precisely because Jesus was one of those privileged by patriarchy that his message is so radical. Jesus' mission announces the end of patriarchy as a divinely-ordained cultural bias. On this reading, "the problem is not that Jesus was a man but that more men are not like Jesus" (p.161) in that they allow their identity to be defined by patriarchy.

Still, this appropriateness does not amount to an ontological necessity. No other aspect of Jesus' being, his race, his class, his social standing, is seen as having ontological significance. Indeed any attempt to do so would severely limit the sweep of salvation, for "what is not assumed is not redeemed." It is not his maleness, but his "loving, liberating history in the midst of the powers of evil and oppression" (p.167) which constitute him as savior. Indeed, Johnson goes so far as to maintain that the present androcentric emphasis on Jesus' maleness, as is found in some arguments against the ordination of women, is heretical and blasphemous.

Thus, despite the maleness of Jesus, Johnson still argues for the application of the female symbol of Sophia to him. The traditional symbols of Son and Word were not indicative of maleness in God, but of a particular type of divine relationality. This same relationality "can be superbly reprised in the symbol of Sophia" (p.166). Indeed, as Johnson notes, the New Testament draws heavily on Sophia symbolism in speaking about Jesus. References to creation being "through him" are taken directly from Wisdom literature. The evocative prologue to John's Gospel is replete with allusions to Sophia, though expressed in the metaphor of *Logos* or Word. And so on throughout the New Testament texts. There should be no doubt that the notion of Jesus as incarnate Sophia is well grounded in the Scriptures.

These are just some of the issues Johnson raises in her profound work. Of further interest are chapters where she contributes to current debates on trinitarian theology and on the suffering of God, taking up concerns we can also see in the works of Jürgen Moltmann and Dorothee Soëlle, both of whom are referred to. Throughout, Johnson maintains a respectful, but not uncritical, stance towards the Christian theological tradition, seeking to bring the valid insights of the past into dialogue with the growing body of feminist reflection and theology. In doing so she has made a significant contribution not simply to feminist theology, but to theology as a whole.

Comments on theological method

As Johnson indicates at the beginning of her work, the fundamental question that this book is seeking to address is, "What is the right way to speak about God?" In light of the preceding decades of feminist thought and theology, in the shadow of women's experience of oppression and domination, how can we speak rightly about God in a way that truly acknowledges that sexism is deeply sinful and destructive of women as *imago Dei*? Throughout her work, Johnson draws on the Scriptures and the Christian theological tradition to uncover resources which can ground an approach which speaks of God in terms of female symbols and female reality. Her strategy is to relativize traditional androcentric language about God and replace it with a solid dose of female language in an attempt to free our imaginations from centuries of patriarchal domination. If women are truly *imago Dei* then it is erroneous to suggest that female language cannot be used of the divine. Indeed it verges on the heretical and the blasphemous.

What is striking is the solid assurance in this work that sexism is sinful. Unlike the earlier feminist theologies, such as that of Ruether, which argued strongly in that direction, here it can confidently be taken for granted. In terms of Lonergan's theological method, we can see that Johnson takes as her starting point the fact of conversion, a conversion away from patriarchy and towards the upholding of the full dignity of women. Anything which detracts from the liberation of women, anything which promotes their oppression or distorts the full reality of the *imago Dei* in women's lives is certainly not from God, is not part of the Gospel, and can be rejected as sin.

Out of conversion grows the functional specialty of foundations and it is here that we see Johnson focusing her theology. Foundations must develop the categories which will allow us to speak of both our religious and secular realities. Traditionally these categories have arisen from men reflecting on male experience. Often these categories contain, sometimes implicitly and sometimes explicitly, androcentric assumptions about the nature of reality, about the meaning of relationship, about what constitutes strength as opposed to weakness, perfection as opposed to fault. Thus the perfection of God is seen in terms of "power over" creation, and in a lack of relatedness to creation. These assumptions are called into question by women's experience which emphasizes empowering above "power over," and the perfection of personal relationship against personal self-sufficiency. Thus in the light of a conversion against patriarchy Johnson develops female symbols and concepts which can promote an alternative vision of the divine, one more congruent with the dignity of women. With a respectful eye towards the past, Johnson ensures that her female categories are well grounded in the tradition, if not explicit within it.

In turn foundations lead to the specialty of doctrines. It is here that Johnson is at her most creative, engaging in a telling exploration of the traditional doctrines of Trinity and divine impassibility (i.e. that God does not suffer). We have already noted her attempts to recast traditional speech about the three persons of the Trinity in female terms. Johnson then pushes this further to uncover the tensions between the traditional language of processions (e.g. the Son *proceeds* from the Father) and the equally traditional language of equality (the Father and Son are one substance). Again women's experience is used to shed new light on these traditional doctrines. Similarly with regard to the question of divine suffering. Johnson is careful to uphold the positive values found in the tradition while raising further questions which it failed to address. Indeed she develops a finely-nuanced account of this issue which maintains a delicate dialectic balance between divine suffering and divine power.

If anything, at this stage Johnson leaves her reader asking for more. As Lonergan's method argues, out of doctrines emerges the need for a systematic. Given the fine work Johnson has done in weaving feminist thought into the doctrine of the Trinity, in what ways will this impact on a systematic theology of the Trinity? Does, for example, the traditional systematic "psychological analogy" need to be recast to move away from its intellectualist foundations to something more grounded in intersubjectivity and personal relationships? Or is it a dying remnant of a patriarchal model of God based on the operations of an isolated divine consciousness? Further, how does feminist speech about divine relationship to the world impact on traditional understandings of the doctrines of grace and incarnation? There is a vast field of further questions which opens up for us as we explore the implications of Johnson's recasting of our categories and doctrines in terms of women's experience. This will perhaps be the next stage for feminist theology.

This, of course, should not be seen as a criticism of the project Johnson has undertaken. Any theological project is of its nature limited. What Johnson has provided is a solid foundation for further feminist theological work. Like the wise scribe she has brought from her storeroom new things as well as old (cf. Matthew 13:52) to illuminate the mystery of God in a feminist key.

CHAPTER 18

Dorothee Soëlle,
A Contemporary Theodicy

Feminist and liberationist themes merge in the writings of Protestant theologian Dorothee Soëlle. Born in Germany and currently living and working there, she also spent over twelve years working in North America. Her writings reflect both cultural contexts, drawing upon experiences with the urban poor in America and peace marches in Germany. Central to her writings are a concern for peace and justice, and particularly the injustice of innocent suffering. As for many German theologians, the Holocaust continues to cast a long shadow over her thinking. As with the writings of Sebastian Moore, her works are a mix of theology and spirituality, though in contrast with his psychological focus, hers is a spirituality of political activism, born of antiwar marches and disarmament rallies.

Out of this struggle has arisen a theological interest in the question of suffering. In particular, where does God stand in relation to human suffering, particularly the suffering of the poor and innocent? Indeed her best known work is simply entitled *Suffering*. In it she provides a powerful critique of what she calls "Christian masochism," which promotes an acceptance of personal suffering, and of Christian apathy towards the suffering of others. In her more recent work, *Theology for Sceptics* she returns to the problem of suffering, only this time with less of a focus on Christians and more of a focus on God. How does God respond to the problems of a suffering humanity? It is to this work that we shall now turn.

Material under consideration—*Theology for Sceptics*, London: Mowbray, 1995

Typically, Soëlle begins her book, not with a text of scripture, or a philosophical reflection on God, but with a simple story, drawn from her own experience, to illustrate our current difficulty in speaking about God. She relates how she sought to engage a young taxi driver in conversation on a trip through Berlin. She broke through his surly silence to find a man full of anger and a sense of hopelessness. Her own attempts to bring God and, with God, a sense of hope into the conversation are met with loud laughter. Reflecting on this experience, she asks why it has become so difficult to speak about God meaningfully when God is, according to Meister Eckhart, "that which is most communicable." For us today the word God is just "too sullied, misused, bandied about, and printed on every dollar, which is probably where it belongs." However, the problem lies not just with the word, God. More fundamentally it is: "About which God are we actually speaking?" (p.9).

It is this question which becomes the key concern of the otherwise loosely-related chapters of this short book. Each chapter invites us to examine this question anew, to explore what sort of God we actually believe in, and what sort of God Jesus represents for us. Drawing on the iconoclastic dimension of her Reformation heritage, Soëlle seeks to break the many idols which seem to resemble God, which act as if they are all-powerful and determining, yet which suck the blood out of people, leaving them blind and caught in evil.

To illustrate her point Soëlle again draws upon stories from her own experience. First there is an account of the Afro-American Vietnam veteran, living in a poor, public housing project in New York city. For him, God is the boss, full of power, authority and command, the one who rules all, who must be "on top." But, notes Soëlle, "it hasn't the least bit to do with justice or mercy" (p.12). Next, the story of the young evangelical woman who declared that Auschwitz was willed by God, because "if God had not willed it, it would not have happened" (pp.13–14). Again the central features of God are power, authority and lordship. Such a view of God, Soëlle argues, makes us impotent nobodies, victims of an inscrutable divine agency beyond our control.

But is this the only way in which we can speak about God? Is this the real God, or is it an idol? Again Soëlle illustrates her point with a story, this time of a young woman struggling to understand the events of the Holocaust, who stated, "When I had understood Auschwitz, I joined the peace movement." For this young woman, and for Soëlle, God "needs people in order to come into being," for without friends, God is powerless. However, in befriending the powerless God, the young woman had found "the strength for resistance, the courage for a clear 'no' in a world that is drunk on the blood of the innocent" (p.15). The contrast between the idolatrous god of power and authority and the real God, who is so often powerless in the face of human evil, is a constant theme of this work.

From this starting point Soëlle launches into a feminist critique of images of God which focus on power, authority and transcendence. Of particular concern is the image of God as father. "Perhaps no image of God is as ambiguous as that of the father, as easy to misuse for authoritarian religion, as easy to harden into obedience and subjection" (p.21). All speech about God as father must be understood in terms of the liberating Kingdom of God that Jesus preached, lest that speech collapse into an authoritarian and sentimental religion devoid of a concern for justice. A symbol which was originally critical of patriarchal culture is now in danger of establishing that culture, to the extent that Soëlle asks, "Does the father image still have any liberating function?" (p.29).

Surprisingly, and unlike some post-Christian feminists, Soëlle can still see a liberating function in the father image:

If talk of God as father helps us not just to accept our dependence as a remnant of earth to be overcome but to affirm it and to accept our finitude and creaturehood, then there is no basis for objecting to this way of speaking. . . . (T)alk of God our Father and God our Mother, can have a liberating effect not because they alleviate the dehumanizing, oppressive characteristics of patriarchy but because they bind us to nature and to the human family (p.31).

Moreover, abolishing the "Father God" will do nothing if it is simply replaced by the "deification of the male," as evidenced in the idolizing of technology, particularly military technology.

The theological difficulty that Soëlle identifies with patriarchy lies not with the use of the father image, or in using male pronouns for God. Rather "patriarchy in its talk about God misses the transcendence of God" (p.37). No name, no symbol is adequate to the reality of God. Any name or symbol which is absolutized becomes then an attack on "God, who is thereby controlled and integrated into the realm of things at one's disposal" (p.38). In particular, symbols of God's omnipotence reveal more about those who use them than about God.

Feminist theology, on the other hand, begins not with the experience of power and control, but with "the experience of being wounded," which shows up patriarchal theology as blind and ignorant. Male theology is revealed as dispassionate, abstract, boring and spiritless. Its God is too small, too trapped in language. With Eckhart, Soëlle prays, "rid me of the God of men" (p.40). Still, the solution is not to replace patriarchy with matriarchy:

> There is controversy on whether the "Goddess" or similar concepts taken mainly from matriarchal culture, like the Great Mother, are productive and liberating or whether with them, as I think, the search is broken off too quickly and we do not carry out Eckhart's leave-taking from God (p.46).

The problem is rather one of overcoming a false transcendence conceived in terms of independence, remoteness and power. Such a God "hardens into a fetish who willed Auschwitz." Such a God is more a Superman, omnipotent, omniscient, omnipresent, expressing "the fatal imperialistic tendency of theology, namely the power of the ruler" (p.49).

These reflections allow Soëlle to return to her main theme, that of a powerless God, a God who suffers with us, and its relationship to the problem of theodicy (that is, of justifying God in the face of innocent suffering). Classical theodicies have attempted to hold together three qualities of God: omnipotence, love and comprehensibility. In fact, Soëlle claims, the history of such arguments proves that these three cannot be held together. Either love is dropped and God becomes an all-powerful sadist who wills Auschwitz; or comprehensibility is lost and God becomes a paradox at best, and at worst, absurd. Or, and this is Soëlle's chosen option, we must drop the idea that God is omnipotent in order to save our faith in God as love. Only a God who suffers with God's creatures can "answer the question of the suffering of the innocent" (p.66).

However, it is not as if Soëlle includes every form of suffering in her quest to understand the suffering of God. It is not a question of God being involved in "every injured vanity, every toothache, every frustration that life inflicts on us" (p.72). Rather we must distinguish between the "sorrow of the world," which produces only death, which knows no hope, and Godly sorrow which "produces a repentance that leads to salvation and brings no regret" (2 Corinthians 7:10). This sorrow arises "from the pain of God over a barbaric world filled with injustice and destruction of life" (p.74). God's pain is the pain of the poor, the abused, the victims of human history. "In El Salvador the pains of the poor are also God's pains. God suffers with them and transforms their pain."

It is this transformation of pain which is God's salvation acting in human history. For though Soëlle distinguishes between the world's pain and Godly pain, they are not unrelated:

> I believe that it is our task to change the "sorrow of the world" into God's pain, and with God's pain, I notice a strange experience. Even though the pain is not tempered, soothed, or denied, it still brings me to a deep joy. ... I am not speaking about a robotic God who will send joy again after pain and sun after rain: I see the sun within the rain. I do not wish to go in search of strength outside of pain; that would be to separate myself from God and to betray God's pain (p.78).

She illustrates her position by reference to the sufferings of a priest working with base Christian communities in Guatemala. Suffering from back-strain from carrying heavy cans of water, the priest offered his suffering "in sacrifice" to Christ.

Soëlle comments on how, once, in her "enlightened Protestant-ism," she saw such a spirituality as abusive and submissive. Now she understands it as a way of seeking to tie the sufferings of our life to God's pain. There is a strength and power to be found in voluntary suffering, which through freedom and sol-idarity with the poor, can become part of God's pain. Yet to appreciate this Soëlle had to overcome the bourgeois individ-ualism present in her Protestant tradition.

In raising the issue of the suffering of God, Soëlle's thought inevitably turns to Jesus Christ, the "man for others," to use Bonhoeffer's phrase. As with her discussion of differing images of God, there are various images of Jesus which she sets out to dispel. In particular there is the image of Jesus as someone from another world, the superhero full of magical powers. For Soëlle such a Christology from above, "which starts with the Godly side of Jesus and makes of him an all-knowing immortal," ends in an heretical Docetism (an early Christological heresy which saw Jesus' humanity as a mere appearance, a mask over his divinity). On such a view of Jesus we can never hope to do what he did. We can never heal the sick, or feed the hungry, so we are absolved from doing anything which could help change the world.

Such a theology is more hero-worship that real Christianity. Soëlle refers to it as "Christolatry" (Christ-idolatry). She rejects the need for heroes and gurus, though not for a redeemer. To reject any such need would be to fall into individualism. Christ is not a hero, but a wounded healer. Drawing upon Søren Kier-kegaard, the Danish philosopher, she makes a distinction between "those who esteem Christ and those who follow him." Those who esteem him have turned Christianity into a person-ality cult "*à la* Joseph Stalin or Adolf Hitler" (p.92), a religion of dependency and impotence.

On the other hand, those who follow Christ are called to solidarity and suffering. When she thinks of Christ, Soëlle thinks "also of Francis of Assisi and Hildegard of Bingen and Martin Luther King Jr., and of Ita Ford, the American nun who was murdered in El Salvador" (p.93). These are people who have let the mysterious power of Christ make them into "fools in Christ," people who, without hope of success or power, share their lives in solidarity with others.

However, there is still the question, why follow this Christ whose life ended in failure, killed like so many others before and after him? Because, as Soëlle struggles to express, "the killing didn't completely work"! (p.94) There is a secret about Jesus which makes him stronger than death and gives those who follow him strength. This secret is not to be found by starting with formulas like "the Anointed One," "Messiah" or "Son of God." Rather its starting point is in the historical reality of Jesus:

> ... the illegitimate son of a poor girl, a teenager; a worker who belonged to the landless; a poor man in every sense of the word, living among the poor, insignificant people, a nobody from a provincial town; a crackpot who was "out of his mind," as his family decided; a subversive who was sought by the authorities; a political prisoner who was tortured and finally condemned to death. . . . (T)he mystery of Christ is the mystery of the suffering, the impoverished, the landless . . . (p.95).

This is the "Christology from below" which Soëlle has learned from the poor of the world.

The Christological formula which best helps Soëlle express her faith is that of Bonhoeffer, who spoke of Christ as the "man for others." This is not to be taken in the sense of a false self-lessness, as is often demanded of women. Indeed Jesus could be very assertive when he had to be. Rather "he was the man-for-others because he was the man of God and knew himself to be ... borne up by God." Soëlle argues that Bonhoeffer's formula "Christ is the man for others" is a valid contemporary expression of the classical Christological formula of the Council of Chalcedon that Christ is "true God" and "true man." "The man for others is the man after God's heart" (p.96).

Thus, in approaching the death and resurrection of Jesus, Soëlle rejects any theology which understands the crucifixion as somehow the result of a divine necessity. God demands no bloody sacrifice to be appeased. Such a God would be a sado-masochistic monster, not the God of Jesus. The cross is about merciless violence against the weak, the poor, the powerless. It is an instrument of torture, used by a military administration, to coerce a subjugated people. It is not God who raised the cross, but Pilate, and all the other Pilates of human history. And it is raised against people who take a stand with the victims of violence, against those who stand for truth and justice. Love has its price. It makes us more vulnerable, more open to attack. It may mean losing friends, careers, lifestyle. But, in the end, we are changed by this love so that "the dead wood of martyrdom begins to turn green. And you know at once where you belong" (p.104).

Given this concrete and political understanding of the crucifixion, Soëlle has no time for academic speculation about the resurrection of Jesus. She finds much of the scholarly discussion off the mark, a "clever diversion from something else, the judicial murder" of Jesus (p.106). We should never isolate the resurrection from the cross. Indeed the resurrection life of Jesus is evident even during his life. "Jesus believed above all—and for all—in a life *before* death" (p.107). This is why they were unable to kill him.

In this brief exposition I hope the reader has got a taste of the powerful mix of feminist, liberationist and political themes operating in Soëlle's writings. They represent a strong challenge to a more conventional, often middle-class, Christian life. They reveal a person of commitment and conviction, but someone who can expose her own vulnerability and struggle in the face of the forces of death present in our culture.

Comments on theological method

Theological works such as Soëlle's are often difficult to categorize. Firstly, they fall into the realm of relatively popular theological works. They are meant to be accessible to the average reader, and presuppose a minimum of theological language and training. Secondly, though the chapters of the book revolve around common themes, they are basically set pieces. Each could appear as a stand-alone article, say, in a journal, without reference to other chapters. There is no systematic development, or working towards a conclusion. Still, there is a fairly natural flow of ideas linking the chapters despite the loose structure.

Another important observation is that, as far as I can tell, Soëlle plays off her theology against that of another leading

German Protestant theologian, Wolfhart Pannenberg (though she makes no mention of him). Where he speaks of the power of God, she talks about powerlessness. Where he sees God the Father as a definitive designation for God, she relativizes the symbol and speaks of God as father and mother. Where he has shown intense interest in the historicity of the resurrection, she feels such questions are a "clever diversion." Having these two together at a dinner party would make for interesting conversation!

Clearly there are deep theological divisions between these two positions. But there is also a difference in theological style or method. Pannenberg's work is most clearly understood as being in the functional specialty of systematics. He seeks a systematic account of the whole of Christian thought. Soëlle's work falls more within the specialty of communications. This is evidenced in her use of story, of poetry, of symbolic and sometimes rhetorical language. It has a direct appeal, much as the Gospels do, to the heart of the listener, and a very particular listener, Western, perhaps middle-class, struggling with what his or her Christian commitment means in a world of the arms race, Third World poverty, trade injustice and violence.

This is clearly Soëlle's strength. Yet it is also her weakness. While it is clear what type of theologies she is reacting against, be it Pannenberg, or a more general tradition, it remains unclear whether and to what extent her own position is open to systematization. It is relatively easy to speak about God's pain, but it is far more difficult to know what it means, and whether it can stand within a systematic account of God as creator, as Trinity, as incarnated in Jesus and so on. There is obviously an implicit metaphysics operating in statements of divine suffering, yet is it coherent with the whole of Christian faith? Again some might question the adequacy of her translation of the faith of Chalcedon into Bonhoeffer's formula of "a man for others." Finally, Soëlle's account of the meaning of the resurrection appears very similar to the theology of Willie Marxsen, that Jesus rises into the life of his disciples. This position has received much criticism from other theologians.

To this extent Soëlle's work is perhaps in need of an appropriate systematic. Nonetheless, it makes a significant contribution by challenging us to break through the many idols which we substitute for the real God. In this she stands in the finest Protestant tradition of protest against the idolatries of our present age.

DISCUSSION QUESTIONS

- In what sense can we speak of the suffering of God? Is it consistent with Christian belief in an all-powerful creator God? Can we reconcile a powerful God with a God vulnerable to suffering?

- Can we call God "mother," as Soëlle suggests, or is there something special about calling God "Father" which can never be changed?

Bibliography

Soëlle has written extensively in the area of feminist, political theology. The following are just some of her works.
Suffering, Philadelphia: Fortress Press, 1974—this is perhaps Soëlle's best known book, dealing, as does *Theology for Sceptics*, with the problem and nature of suffering.
Political Theology, Philadelphia: Fortress Press, 1974—Soëlle argues that political theology is not a new subdivision within theology but the basic form of theology. She draws extensively on the theology of Rudolph Bultmann to develop her position.
To Work and To Love—A Theology of Creation, Philadelphia: Fortress Press, 1984.
The Window of Vulnerability, Minneapolis: Fortress Press, 1990.
Thinking About God, Philadelphia/London: Trinity Press/SCM, 1990—this work looks at the major themes of Christian theology through the eyes of Soëlle's Feminist Political Theology.

CHAPTER 19

John Meyendorff, *Orthodox Theology*

For many Christians in the Western tradition, Orthodox Christianity remains an esoteric, distant and culturally–distinct form of Christian life and theology. The Western experience of Orthodoxy is often one of cultural and ethnic minorities struggling to maintain an identity which appears to Western eyes as a relatively undifferentiated mix of religious, cultural and social values. To read Orthodox theology, in particular, is to enter into a different world, a world of quite different thought patterns, authorities, and concerns from those that have dominated the Western theological tradition. Put simply, there was no Augustine and no Reformation in the East!

Still, it is a tradition towards which more Western theologians, both Catholic and Protestant, are turning. In Catholic thought it has often been through the influence of a renewal of Patristic thought, as evidenced in the *nouvelle théologie* of the forties and fifties. In particular the theme of deification, so prominent in the Greek Fathers and so important to contemporary Orthodoxy, was taken up by theologians such as Karl Rahner. Among Protestants, Orthodoxy has represented an alternative metaphysical approach for theology to the Catholic Scholasticism which they have consistently rejected. This has been most evident in the area of trinitarian theology, particularly among English-speaking authors.

John Meyendorff is a leading and internationally-respected Orthodox theologian and priest. He has written extensively on theological topics, generally from an historical perspective, an approach characteristic of all Orthodox theology. At the heart of Orthodox theology is a profound respect for tradition, especially the tradition as represented by the early Greek Fathers of the Church. To read such theology is to see these figures come alive, to understand the passion of their concerns, to appreciate the depth of their Christian vision.

However, Meyendorff has not just been an "academic" theologian, studying, writing and teaching. He has been deeply involved in the ecumenical movement, taking part in discussion in the World Council of Churches and even chairing, at one time, the Faith and Order Commission of the WCC. He has also reflected on the current plight of Orthodoxy in the modern world, the challenges it faces and the reforms it must undertake. Throughout the writings we shall consider, Meyendorff is critical not only of what he sees as Western, and particularly Roman, ecclesial distortions, but also the failure of the Orthodox Churches to live out the ecclesiology they hold. In his own way his has been a theology of praxis, of active engagement in the issues which his theology has illuminated.

Material under consideration—*Living Tradition*, Crestwood, N.Y.: St Vladimir's Seminary Press, 1978

The book, *Living Tradition*, is a collection of occasional essays and addresses written from 1958 to 1975, gathered around the theme of the relationship between Orthodoxy and the modern world, both secular and ecclesial. The title is indicative of a concern central to Orthodox theology and life, that of Tradition. In the Orthodox perspective, Tradition is a living vibrant reality, not something from the past to be repeated by rote. It finds its basis, not in an appeal to authority, either in the Church or in the Scriptures, but in the living presence of the Holy Spirit guiding all believers to the fullness of Truth. Tradition is a "living and organic reality manifesting the presence of the Spirit in the Church" (p.26). Through revelation grounded in the life of the Spirit, people participate in the divine life, something which is witnessed in the Scriptures and experienced in the sacramental life of the Church.

According to Meyendorff, the Orthodox understanding of Tradition is significantly different from that of the West. The basic difference between Orthodoxy and the West is "a conflict of 'authority' in religion" (p.27). What is at stake in this conflict is the very concept of authority in matters of faith, not only who or what holds authority. While Catholics locate authority in the papal office and Protestants locate it in the Scriptures, Orthodoxy sees God alone as authoritative, not however as an extrinsic reality to the Church, but as a living presence through the Spirit. Jesus is present through the Spirit so that the Church community is truly the "Body of Christ." Because of this, any authority vested in particular persons, such as Peter or the Apostles, "can only be an authority within the community, and not *over* it" (p.31). Indeed, Meyendorff argues that there can never be any human authority over the People of God.

Of course this is not to deny the role of the episcopacy in the life of the Church. Like Catholicism, Orthodoxy has a hierarchical, episcopal ecclesiology. Citing Irenaeus, an early Church Father, Meyendorff argues that the episcopacy is an expression of the sacramental nature of the community, not of power or authority over the community. "Sacramental life, especially the Eucharist, requires the Church to be internally structured and hierarchical" (p.33). While individual bishops have a teaching role, they do not possess a personal infallibility. "His teachings and opinions must be checked and compared with those of his colleagues elsewhere" (p.36). Even when a large number of bishops are gathered, as in a Church Council, there is needed a process of "reception" of any decrees by the whole Church before they are considered authoritative. The Church cannot impose truth on our minds. Rather it can help us "live and grow in the Spirit" so that we can "see and experience the Truth" for ourselves (p.41).

In making these comments it is clear that Meyendorff has Rome in his sights. In an essay entitled "Rome and Orthodoxy: Is 'Authority' Still the Issue?" (pp.63–79), he summarizes the sad and sorry history of the schism between West and East. He notes recent efforts to heal the break, in particular the mutual "lifting the anathemas" of 1054 (the time of the historic break between East and West), but argues that such moves will remain largely symbolic unless there is some lasting solution to the problem of authority within the Church. What is needed on both sides is "a common frame of reference in terms of Church *authority*" (p.69). While Orthodoxy is prepared to accept the Pope as "first among equals," they also insist on an ontological equality between all bishops, which opposes claims of primacy and the centralisation of dogmatic authority and legal power. This opposition would require a reevaluation of Catholic doctrines such as the *filioque* (that the Holy Spirit proceeds from the Father *and the Son*, in Latin, *filioque*), the Assumption of Mary and the Immaculate Conception of Mary. These doctrines "should not be seen as possessing universal validity" (p.75), contrary to present Catholic claims.

Meyendorff argues that the West's reliance on authority to solve its religious disputes "creates a religious void wherever authority weakens or disappears" (p.78). The void created by the breakdown in religious authority occasioned by the Enlightenment has led the Churches to "humanistic activism and secularism." On the other hand, the rich liturgical experience so central to Orthodox religious life has allowed them to escape such difficulties.

Indeed the Orthodox have a much richer understanding of liturgy than the West. For Orthodoxy the liturgy is a foretaste of the eschatological Kingdom to come:

> Liturgical worship is indeed the leisure, the "going home" of Christians inasmuch as they are through their baptism the citizens of the Kingdom of God, not of the world. The anticipated eschatology of the Eucharist is a relief, the very experience of a victory already won . . . (p.144).

As such, the Eucharist is not an escape from reality but an escape from the necessities and determinisms of the world, an escape from the "principalities and powers" which can dominate our existence. In the Eucharist the eschatological Kingdom is anticipated in the life of the local Church community. Indeed Meyendorff argues that only those Church structures which have such an eschatological dimension are necessary. While obviously accepting the necessity of a hierarchical episcopacy, he seriously questions whether the papal office, as "vicar of

Christ" or "successor to Peter" is required by the eschatological nature of the Eucharist.

This issue of eschatology is raised again in one of the final essays in this collection, "The Christian Gospel and Social Responsibility." In this Meyendorff compares three different eschatological types. The first sees the "Kingdom" as arriving through a sudden, cataclysmic divine intervention into human history, usually in "a not-so-distant future." He rejects this approach because it "provides no basis for any Christian mission to society or to culture" (p.189). It is an eschatology of withdrawal which leaves no room for legitimate human effort and aspirations. The second eschatological type goes in the opposite direction, "based on a belief in the never-ending progress of human society" (p.189) through dint of hard work and scientific advancement. Meyendorff describes this approach as Pelagian, a reference to an early heresy of the Church. He sees this type as promoting the very historical determinism from which Christianity is meant to free us.

The third and correct eschatological type "does justice both to God's power and to man's freedom and responsibility" (p.190). Biblical eschatological prophecy is, according to Meyendorff, never a matter of strict inevitability or foretelling. Rather it is conditional, holding out the possibility of either promise or menace. It is a matter of human freedom as to whether the second coming of Jesus "will be a frightful judgment or a joyous marriage feast for him and for his society" (p.190).

Meyendorff argues that in general the West has opted for the second of these eschatologies. This in turn is based on a flawed secular anthropology which understands the human person as autonomous, independent from, and complete without, the divine. He does not object to the modern anthropological turn within theology, so long as the anthropological base is adequate to the Christian mystery. For examples he refers to the writings of another Orthodox theologian, Vladimir Loosky, who argues that "no Christian ecclesiology . . . is possible on the basis of a secularized anthropology, which necessarily reduces the Church to the level of a human organization" (p.135).

In this regard Meyendorff makes several positive references

to the work of Karl Rahner and his "theocentric" anthropology. Such an anthropology is very sympathetic to the Orthodox notion of deification (*theosis*) which is so central to their spirituality, and he sees Rahner as an influential ally in the West. Perhaps at the time of writing Meyendorff was unaware of how great that influence was to become, for Rahner's anthropology has become a theological staple for many Catholic theologians.

The criticisms Meyendorff levels at the West, both Catholic and Protestant, should not be taken to indicate that all is rosy within the Orthodox world. In fact he is very strongly critical of various aspects of Orthodoxy. He accepts that "the Orthodox East has often been too contemplative and (why hide it?) somehow monophysite" (p.95) and that it has often suffered from a "confusion between Church and civilization, religion and nation" (p.156). However, his strongest criticisms are for the failure of Orthodoxy to live out the unity which it professes as part of its identity.

The most glaring example of this failure, according to Meyendorff, is America (though similar observations could be made about Australia and Britain), where a number of Orthodox Churches exercise jurisdiction over the same geographical domain:

> One question, however, requires action more urgently than any other, the local or "territorial" principle of church life and administration. There cannot exist any doctrinal, disciplinary, missionary, or canonical justification for the state of canonical chaos in which the Orthodox Church lives, for example, in America (p.105).

The jurisdictional separation of Orthodox churches into Greek, Ukrainian, Russian, Serbian and so on means that the Church is "unable to fulfill its mission, for it is formally exclusive of those who do not belong to its ethnicity" (p.106). Such a position was formally rejected as heretical (referred to as "phyletism") by Orthodoxy in 1872 in a council held at Constantinople (Istanbul), yet it is still tolerated in America. Meyendorff notes that if Irish, Polish and Italian Catholics can be united in one Church, why must the Orthodox be separated on ethnic lines? Indeed, "the Church must manifest its visible God-established unity" (p.107) as a community open to all and transcending merely cultural values and ethnic identity.

Coupled with this is a need to review Church canon law. Orthodoxy has never had a codified law as exists within Catholicism and so is often faced with a variety of compilations of varying significance and validity. Some are practically ignored while others are treated as having universal validity. As with so many other Churches, there are fundamentalists who want all enforced, and liberals who reject any notion of canon law at all. Meyendorff argues for the pedagogical value of law and its theological, as opposed to purely legal, significance. Still there are issues that need to be faced, especially those concerning the elevation of married men to the episcopacy (forbidden, but ignored by some), the possibility of marriage after ordination (Orthodoxy will ordain married men, but those ordained single are to remain celibate), and the possibility of ordination for those divorced and remarried.

Finally Orthodoxy must reassess it relationship to its own past. Here Meyendorff confronts the key tension of particularity versus universality. The Orthodox claim to be the universal catholic Church, yet they are tied to a particular cultural and historical tradition, the great Tradition of the Greek Fathers. This Tradition has its own history, its own rootedness, through a variety of Christian empires and domains. This history cannot simply be left behind or abandoned, but ultimately the "Church . . . cannot be 'Eastern' or 'Western' . . . if it is to remain the Church of Christ" (p.160).

So Orthodoxy must get its own house into order, according to Meyendorff. It faces a number of pressing issues: of canon law, of mission, of its weddedness to ethnic and cultural identity, and to a world view where Church and state work together for the promotion of a "Christian" society. While fully committed to the vision of Christian life that Orthodoxy promotes, Meyendorff is clearly not blind to the difficulties it faces. Still, not only the Orthodox, but also we of the West, have much to learn from this leading theologian.

Comments on theological method

It is difficult and perhaps a bit unfair to attempt to make some comments on the theological approach of material which by its very nature is occasional and varied. The essays in this book were often papers given to address concerns of particular audiences and so we do not find in them a sustained engagement with serious theological issues. Rather, we have an intense but brief engagement with a large variety of questions which the author deals with expeditiously. The other difficulty lies in the fact that there is little explicit concern with methodological questions, especially in comparison with the sophisticated methodological question with which Western theology is currently struggling. The critico-historical approach to the Scriptures, so central to contemporary theology in the West, seems to have played little to no role in the East. The "search for the historical Jesus" is not an issue, though the "search for the historical Nestorius" is (see, for example, Meyendorff's *Christ in Eastern Christian Thought*, Crestwood, New York: St Vadimir's Seminary Press, 1975, p.18, esp. n.7).

It is not, of course, that Meyendorff's theology is historically uncritical. Indeed, it is highly critical. However, the focus of that methodological approach does not expand so as to encompass the Scriptures. One feels at times that, for Orthodoxy, Christianity began in the fourth century. Still, the historical concern is strong, indeed vital, in understanding Meyendorff's theological method.

However, it does not end with history. Meyendorff's approach is also highly dialectical. Protestantism, Catholicism and Orthodoxy represent differing and divergent historical options on fundamental questions of authority and ecclesiology. This divergence amounts to a dialectical opposition, whereby what one values as good and right the other rejects as bad and wrong. Meyendorff illustrates such an opposition in his rejection of Western reliance on authority at the expense of the religious experience of the living Spirit in the Church. Indeed he points us to the importance of conversion by highlighting the role of liturgy in Orthodox life. The Eucharist is the locus of Christian conversion, the central experience around which the whole Christian life is organized. In so doing his work emphasises the *ecclesial* context of conversion, a feature common amongst Orthodox theologians.

Conversion moves us onto the question of foundations, and it is here that we see some of the limitations of Meyendorff's work. Such a move requires a shift from historical questions into more philosophical concerns. Meyendorff himself identifies the key role played by opposed anthropologies in the dialectics above, and points the reader in the direction of the "theocentric" anthropology of Rahner for a possible way forward. Indeed for much contemporary Catholic theology Rahner's work has provided such a foundational base. Still, this is not an area which Meyendorff himself explores in this work. However, as Lonergan has argued, theology is a collaborative enterprise and this limitation should not be seen as a weakness.

Meyendorff also points us in the direction of the doctrines which are so central to Orthodox life. In a Western culture in which religious doctrines appear so often as the discarded remnants of dogmatic authoritarianism and superstition, Orthodoxy continues to "affirm and describe the divine, eternal, and absolute truths of Orthodox theology about God, Christ, and the Church" (p.82). There are central truths which the Church cannot ignore without ceasing to be itself. Error and heresy remain problems because they have a deadening effect on human life; they betray the fullness of truth to which the Gospels bear witness, the fullness of life we are called to live.

Still, we can share a smile with our author when he describes Orthodoxy as "the right faith held by the wrong people" (p.83). As always there is a gap between theory and praxis, between orthodoxy and orthopraxis, not only in the Orthodox Church, but among all Christians. We all know that orthodox belief is no guarantee of right actions, though this is never to say that it is simply of no value. It becomes the gauge by which we measure our own failures.

Orthodox theology is an important tradition of theologizing which the West is slowly rediscovering. The works of John Meyendorff, John Zizioulas and Kallistos Ware, to name a few, have done much to bring its riches to light and make it available to Western theologians. The work *Living Tradition* by Meyendorff is an excellent entry point for anyone seeking a taste of its theological approach.

DISCUSSION QUESTIONS

● Would you agree with Meyendorff's assessment that Western Christianity is too concerned with the issue of authority?

● Have you experienced an Eastern Orthodox liturgy? How does it compare with a Western liturgy? How important is the experience of the liturgical life of a community to understanding the theology of that community?

Bibliography

John Meyendorff has written a number of works dealing with theological questions from an Orthodox perspective. The following may be of interest.
Byzantine Theology, London: Mowbrays, 1974—this work considers a number of theological questions from an Orthodox perpective.
Christ in Eastern Christian Thought, New York: St Vladimir's Seminary Press, 1975—a difficult work to get into without substantial background in the Christological debates in the fourth and fifth centuries. However, Meyendorff makes the characters of this historical period come alive.
Marriage: An Orthodox Perspective, New York: St Vladimir's Seminary Press, 1975—an Orthodox approach to marriage, a tradition which differs from the Catholic approach on some central issues.
    The following works may also be of interest.
K., Ware, *The Orthodox Way*, London: Mowbrays, 1981—this work could be described as an Orthodox catechism, a good introduction to Orthodox belief.
J., Zizioulas, *Being as Communion*, London: Darton, Longman and Todd, 1985—Zizioulas' work in this book has done much to bring orthodox trinitarian theology into dialogue with Western approaches.

Conclusion

At this stage, it might be of value to make some concluding comments about the state of play in contemporary theology. As can be seen from this book, contemporary theology is dealing with questions and issues which are quite different from those of preceding theological eras. Moreover, these questions and issues are being handled with methodologies unknown to the past. It is the methodological question which I believe is crucial to contemporary theology. It is for this reason that I have used the methodological approach of Bernard Lonergan, with his eight functional specialties and four conversions. If nothing else, I hope that this work can illustrate the utility of his method for both uniting and criticizing the diversity of approaches used by the theologians considered in this book.

As theology comes to reflect more on the methodological question, it will be more able to break free from the dogmatic authoritarianism which seeks to suppress theological research. For such authoritarianism, truth is always "in possession"—it appears from nowhere, without history, without origin, except of course in God. It is to be found by simply "looking" at scripture or tradition. A methodologically aware theology will know that such a position is hermeneutically naive, that it is forever in danger of subsiding over into fideism. A methodologically aware theology will know that truth lives in the hearts, minds and deeds of believers, and that these are the ultimate carriers of the Christian faith.

However, such a theology, if it is not to subside into a weak liberalism, allowing every position as part of a "legitimate pluralism," must also find a place for the definitive, the truth, carried in the hearts, minds and deeds of believers, but expressed in the definitive judgments of the past. It seems to me that such a position cannot be denied. Even those theologians who avoid doctrines, in following the dynamism of their own faith, arrive at "doctrines" of their own. Like a denial of knowledge, a denial of dogma becomes self-defeating—in its own way it becomes a new dogma!

I hope this work has helped readers find a balance between the apparently competing claims of theological research and fidelity to the tradition. If so it has more than served its purpose.

*   *   *

Since the first edition of this book there have been some momentous events, at least in the life of the Catholic community. In the last few years we have seen the introduction of the "Oath of Fidelity," the publication of the *Catechism of the Catholic Church*, the issuing of several encyclicals, most notably *Veritatis Splendor* on moral issues, and an apostolic letter on the ordination of women. These are clear indications that the dialectic tension between authority and research, between tradition and innovation, is swinging back in the direction of authority and tradition. Still, it is difficult to gauge the long-term impact of this shift. Some theologians simply no longer care what position ecclesiastical authority adopts. Others are dealing with issues, such as theology and ecology, on which the tradition has little to say.

There is no magic formula which will return the genie of theological pluralism back into its bottle. Nor is such a return obviously desirable. We have much to learn from the present pluralism, but only if our theological methodology is adequate to the task.

While the above comments relate particularly to the situation of Catholic theologians, in the world of academic theology such a distinction means little. Catholics, Protestants, Orthodox are all one theological community, reading, analyzing and commenting on one another's work. Because of this, any major shift in the Catholic community will inevitably impact upon all theologians. Hopefully this new edition, with its inclusion of some Protestant and Orthodox theologians, will give the reader a deeper sense of the commonality of the theological task across differing Church communities.

Index of Names

Anselm 3, 5, 10, 77
Aquinas 5, 6, 7, 10, 15, 18, 28-29, 55,
    79, 84, 94, 99, 101, 103-104, 111,
    114, 135-136, 177, 185
Arius 136
Aristotle 17, 18, 28, 79, 84, 87, 111,
    137
Augustine 9, 17, 55, 73, 101, 135,
    138, 177, 185

Balthasar, H.U. v. 45
Barth, K. 4, 21, 31, 34, 45-46, 61, 67,
    92, 109, 134, 135, 177
Becker, E. 72-73, 78
Benedict XV 10, 37-8
Bergson, H. 24
Birch, C. 24
Bloch, E. 134
Boff, L. 141-142, 149, 154-163, 188
Bonhoeffer, D. 201
Buber, M. 39
Bultmann, R. 22, 35, 92, 204

Calvin, J. 137
Camus, A. 22
Chirico, P. 40, 115
Cobb, J. 24

Darwin, C. 34-35, 128
Doellinger, I. 36
Dulles, A. 43, 45, 46-47, 53

Eckhart 196, 198
Eliot, T.S. 74

Fichte 20, 97
Freud, S. 23, 39, 72, 79, 183

Gadamer, H. 23
Gutiérrez, G. 22, 144-153

Habermas, J. 23
Harnack, A. v. 32
Hegel, G.F. 20-21, 24, 35, 92, 126
Heidegger, M. 22, 92, 104
Hume, D. 65

Ignatius of Antioch 137
Irenaeus 131, 207

Joachim of Fiore 139-140
John XXIII 62, 116
John Paul II 8, 148
Johnson, E. 185-194
Jung, C.G. 39, 79, 181, 188

Kant, E. 18-20, 21, 25, 35, 39, 46,
    52-53, 85, 89, 92, 103-104,
    106-107, 114, 140, 145
Kierkegaard, S. 35, 200
Küng, H. 21, 61-70, 71, 81, 88, 106,
    159, 161

Lamb, M. 115
Leenhardt, F.J. 85
Leo XIII 83
Lonergan, L. 10-11, 16, 20, 35, 50,
    52-53, 56, 88, 100, 111, 114-123,
    172, 192-193, 213

Loosky, V. 209
Luther, M. 5, 35, 78, 86, 177

Macquarrie, J. 22
Maréchal, J. 103-104
Marx, K. 20, 21-22, 23, 144, 145, 147, 150-151, 183
Marxen, W. 203
Metz, J. 35, 54, 112, 124-133, 182
Meyendorff, J. 205-214
Mölher, H. 31
Moore, S. 35, 54, 71-80, 109, 115, 195
Moltmann, J. 24, 92, 134-143, 191

Newman, J.H. 31
Nietzsche, F. 23
Novak, M. 150

Ogden, S. 24
Origen 98
Orsy, L. 115

Pannenberg, W. 15, 24, 44, 92-102, 134, 203
Peterson, E. 130-131, 159
Pius X 33
Pius XII 36
Plato 17, 28, 89, 98

Rahner, K. 5, 20, 21, 22, 35, 38-39,

54, 61, 79, 103-113, 124-126, 129, 131, 135-136, 205, 210, 213
Ratzinger, J. 125, 159
Riceour, P. 23
Robinson, J. 95
Ruether, R. Radford 175-184, 185, 187, 189, 192

Sabellius 136
Sartre, J.P. 22
Schelling 20
Schillebeeckx, E. 67, 81-91, 160, 161
Schleiermacher, F. 31, 92
Schnackenberg, R. 159
Schooenberg, P. 116, 122
Schüssler Fiorenza, E. 164-174, 176-177, 182, 185
Schweitzer, A. 36, 37
Scotus, Duns 92
Soëlle, D. 141, 191, 195-204

Tertullian 4, 46
Teilhard de Chardin, P. 35
Tillich, P. 15, 22, 52, 95
Tracy, D. 23, 24, 115

Ware, T. 213
Whitehead, A. 24, 35, 92

Zizioulas, J. 213